A
Pinch
Of
Saltee

HENRY GRATTAN BELLEW

A PINCH OF SALTEE

ISBN 1-900913-09-7

A CIP catalogue for this book is available
from the British Library

First published in 2003 by
Justin Nelson Productions.
www.iol.ie/~jnelson/

Available for purchase on the Little Saltee website
http://homepage.eircom.net/~snicholson

A PINCH OF SALTEE

For Deirdre

*my beloved sister who regrettably
never made the trip.*

A PINCH OF SALTEE

CONTENTS

Acknowledgements
Foreword
Outline Map
Prologue

A PINCH OF SALTEE

A PINCH OF SALTEE

ACKNOWLEDGEMENTS

I am greatly indebted to the following for all their assistance.

Greg, Philomena and Rory Stafford, John Devereux, Declan Bates, Billy Bates, Dave Sumray with Jacqui, Lewin and Molly, John, Anna and David Bland, George Culleton, Finbar Buttimer, Ivan Ward, Raymonde Hilliard, Michael O'Connor, Dan Gubbins and Staff, David Cabot, Tommy McLoughlin, Marty Scallan, Eugene Wallace, Chas Bates, Mary and Josephine Doyle, Nick and Josie Power, Seamus Cowman, Kevin Casey, Paddy Barry, Bobby Stafford, Jackie Connick, Bodie Bates, Eamon Mooney, Percy Podger, Sean and Pauline Ennis, Cyril Green and Bob Killen and their expert and jovial staff.

The staff of Kehoe's Pub, the Upper Deck, the Quay Plaice and Kehoe's Hardware. The gentle people at Creevy's Store, Murphy's (formerly Hogans), and Tony our friendly butcher.

Brian Kehoe and his amazing voluntary staff aboard the RNLI *Mary Margaret*.

All the lobsterboat men whom we befriended and who keep a watchful eye on island, boats and livestock.

The Harbour Master, Capt. Eddie Barratt, his assistants Johnny Synnott and Peter Devereux who run the marina in exemplary fashion.

The various members of the Agricultural Department at Enniscorthy, Co. Wexford. Some who remain behind desks and others who brave the elements.

A PINCH OF SALTEE

Mickey Strong, a 'Harvey' like character, who was always there when needed. Almost invisible, his recipe for success was never far from my senses.

A very special vote of gratitude to Susan Byrne (Cabinteely Writing Classes) who kick started me into putting pen to paper originally and then to John Kelly and his Writers Workshop class of 2002/2003 (Newpark Comprehensive School) whose enthusiasm and guidance made it all happen.

George and Shelia Kiely and Emjie Baird who religiously read and corrected every chapter proffering advice with encouragement. Words of gratitude fail me. To Valerie Stevenson for her endless assistance whenever our computer had the sulks or contacted a virus. Our canine companion, Oscar. His presence during this entire half decade gave such joy. His smile and wagging tail brought happiness and delight aplenty.

And finally, Shirley - my lighthouse – who not only matched me step for step on the island, but who typed and retyped every word, time and again as I re-edited the novella. Her patience and skill on the computer, not only in putting 'A Pinch' together but for also designing and creating our Little Saltee web site, with its annual update, are priceless.

There are many things I have been able to tackle and contest convincingly but sitting in front of a computer is not one of them. My gratitude, therefore, is immeasurable. I must humbly apologise for making you an island widow, instead of me being a golf widower!!

As the late great Barry White used to croon 'She's my first. She's my last. She's my everything'.

FOREWORD

God loves a dreamer

I first met Henry Grattan Bellew when he was hunting a thoroughbred horse over the stonewalls of County Galway. He proceeded to tell me he planned for the horse to win the Joseph O Reilly in Fairyhouse and the La Touche in Punchestown, Ireland's top two hunter chases. Like others at the time I thought Henry, along with many horse owners, was suffering from an inflated opinion of his horse's ability and told him to "dream on". We subsequently had many great days at point to points and race meetings cheering on the horse "Metalwood" who delivered on Henry's dream! While another person might be hoping for a win in the adjacent hunts race at their local point to point, not our Henry. I have no doubt that had the horse not suffered a tendon injury that terminated his racing career Henry's next goal of having a crack at the Grand National in Aintree would have been realised.

Subsequently I encountered Henry when he was carving a 6,000 acre cereal farm out of the bush adjacent to his home farm on the Maasai Mara in Kenya. He had an airstrip on the farm for the crop spraying aeroplanes and this doubled as his grass gallops. From his base in the Mara he used to take his horses for periodic raids into Nairobi racecourse where he regularly held court. On the farm he had built a replica Irish thatched cottage, complete with half door, just in case he was feeling home sick. He was, and still is, a fantastic host, and the farm was used by many as a base for exploring the Mara and his racehorses were regularly used for horseback safaris.

On returning to Ireland his next project was to turn his beloved Little Saltee into the magical place it has become. In Shirley he has found a soul mate who appears like him to have defied the ageing process. Their "Can do" positive attitude puts many younger people to shame.

A PINCH OF SALTEE

Both of them love a challenge and this story captures the excitement and enthusiasm associated with their adventures on the Little Saltee. The fun and pleasure they have enjoyed with this project should be an example to us all that life is for living and one should never throw in the towel. Many people set themselves targets and put their lives on hold obsessed with achieving these. Henry's motto "to enjoy the journey in case you never arrive at your destination" is one that many of us would do well to adopt.

I thought Henry's eternal optimism would be dented when he suffered a heart attack while holidaying in South Africa and he required a quadruple cardiac by pass. But his response when I met him on his return to Ireland typifies the man, " I felt great before I had the operation now I'll surely be a hero"!

I think when God made Henry Grattan Bellew he destroyed the mould. Probably Society couldn't handle another like him.

Dr. Patrick Wall
Centre for Food Safety
University College Dublin

A PINCH OF SALTEE

OUTLINE MAP, CIRCA 1998, LITTLE SALTEE ISLAND

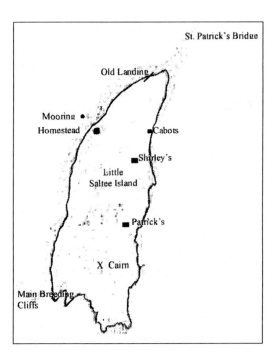

Approaching the island from Kilmore Quay

A PINCH OF SALTEE

PROLOGUE

My promise was made on the harbour wall of Kilmore Quay, Co. Wexford. Grandpa was too old, he said, to come out with my sister Deirdre and I in Willie Bates' small boat. He would go off for a drive with his chauffeur. It was a glorious summer's day and very calm as Willie set off for what, for us, was quite an adventure. He was taking us out to the Little Saltee Island which my Grandparents owned. We could see the two islands very clearly as we left the harbour entrance. The Little Saltee, from that distance, looked rather like half an emergent whale. The bigger island reminded my sister of her pony Fergus who had a sway back. I sort of saw the likeness!

On the way out we noticed a strange 'meeting of waters' to our left which Willie told us was called St. Patrick's Bridge. In folk lore it was said that St. Patrick had been chasing the devil out of Ireland. When he saw all the water in front of him he kept throwing stones until he could walk on top of them and reach the island. Evidently at low tide one still could almost wade out along it from the mainland. That's what helped the farmers get their implements and animals out to the island, he said.

The little engine, I think it was a Seagull, gently pushed our open boat along the intervening distance, which we learnt was approximately three miles between the mainland and the Little Saltee. Soon we moored off the island on the west side and Willie cut the engine. We then drifted with the tide or current which he said was very strong close to the shore. Willie told us that the brothers White, William and Richard, were our tenant farmers on it. The island farm looked serene, so peaceful in a world that was at war. We could see the farm buildings, homestead, cattle, sheep and a couple of horses. Fields of golden corn shone in the late morning sunshine. We also saw men working in the fields. They were stooking[1] the corn which was being harvested. Chickens or fowl of

---

[1] Stacking bundles of corn into vertical formations

some kind were active around the homestead because we heard the odd crowing and cock-a doodle-doing. Thousands of seabirds flew hither and thither.

After circling the island Willie brought us back on the eastern side of St. Patrick's Bridge. The white horses that made this artistic phenomena was due to the tides meeting right along the bridge. It was calm where Willie took us. We were loath to be returning so soon.

"Did you enjoy that children?" asked Grandpa when we landed safely back in the little harbour.

"Yes, indeed", said I with great glee and wonderment. Deirdre said she liked the horses and the birds but questioned why there were no trees on the island.

"That's because the islands are lashed by violent storms in the winter months", Grandpa explained. He thanked Mr. Bates for his services and time. So did we.

As it was so warm and sunny we ate our picnic on the little beach beside the harbour wall. Deirdre and I swam. It was shallow and quite warm. Lots of others were also swimming and enjoying the summer sunshine.

We walked back to the car. As we looked out across the blue waters to the islands Grandpa put his arm around me and said:

"Promise me, one day, you will farm that island".

I looked at him in amazement. Simply replying "Yes Sir, I promise"

I sat in the back seat with Grandpa on our return trip to Tinnahinch, Enniskerry, Co. Wicklow. This was the home which the 'people of Ireland' had given to Henry Grattan M.P. for services rendered. He was my distant grandpa. Deirdre sat up front with Larkin the chauffeur. Not a lot was said. We were all tired. I had loved Kilmore Quay and all the thatched cottages. The boat ride, the islands, the birds, the ice cream. That day became imprinted on my mind for decades to come. I wanted to return. Both Grandpa and Grandma died a few years later. It had been a magical day, August 17th, 1941.

A PINCH OF SALTEE

Chapter One

Little Saltee – Ballytrent – Kenya Colony – The Quay – Mill Road

In was now1998 some fifty-seven years later. Major changes had taken place in Kilmore Quay. They now had a well walled non-tidal harbour with a vibrant marina. The view out to the island, however, remained virtually the same. St. Patrick's Bridge had two coloured buoys, one red, one green, halfway along its two and a half mile curving waistline of waves and white horses. These marked a deep water channel which had been blown out of the rock formation to allow trawlers and large yachts to pass through without any problems. A dozen or so trawlers, now resident in Kilmore Quay, made a formidable fishing fleet. Yachts of all sizes, colours and nationalities filled the marina. I again sensed that special fishy smell that harbours universally hold but now it was tainted with dieseline. Not a friendly aroma.

Shirley and I had been away in India for the past three years so we were impatient to visit and see the birds on the island.

This time it was Declan Bates who took us out. He towed a punt behind Tapaidh, the boat he used for ferrying birders and photographers out to the big island. Old Willie, Declan's father, had passed away in 1986. Declan had then personally taken over the tourist segment of the family empire as well as running three trawlers two of which were captained by his sons. It was another fine day. The water was calm and we were very thankful for this as we might not yet have our sea legs! He moored about fifty metres off the little island on the western side almost opposite the farm buildings as Tapaidh could not approach any nearer for fear of hitting rocks. We then got into the little punt with Declan and he took us safely onto the shoreline. That, I remembered, had looked a dangerous and daunting area. One that would amass gigantic problems for us in the years to come. The tide was about halfway out which offered up a twenty metre square area of sandy beach between the rocks.

We spent approximately five hours out on our plot of paradise that day. It was mid summer. Bracken[2] had taken over the place. It was tall and tough to walk through. Only the field above and next to the old ruin of the homestead was bare of it. This we investigated. It was bare of grass. It had become a giant rabbit warren. Right then it also housed hundreds of seagulls' nests. Light amber and blue spotted eggs nestled in sparsely created indentations in the ground. Hardly a step could be taken without having to negotiate a clutch of two or three. Almost Tern-like these large Black-backed and Lesser Black-backed screechers dive bombed us menacingly close whilst goading us on. Gull sentinels stood atop the eight gable ends of the roofless buildings. Walls were well soiled.

The entire island is divided into fields by Connemara styled granite stone walls. A lot of these had subsided quantifiably since the tenants departed in 1946. Some, however, with ditches on one side still made quite formidable fences. A number of them had been taken over as nesting areas for Cormorants.

We walked the hundred acres extensively noting the various seabirds amidst their nesting grounds. This was their busy time. Razor Bills seemed to be in the majority. Thousands of these squat black and white divers stood statuesquely on our southern cliffs. Their distinctive white-lined beaks slightly grinning at us as we, ashamedly, disturbed them. Puffins were very active both on land near the cliff edges and in the sea below. One could best describe them as comical in looks and flight. Their bills of red, yellow and blue bands mixed and matched with other black, white, yellow and orange parts of their bodies. It would need a book in itself to concentrate on all the different species. We found three water holes covered in watercress. I tried some. It tasted tart and sandy like I remembered in sandwiches made by my

---

[2] Fern

nanny many years ago. Five raucous colourful cock pheasants flew out ahead of us disturbing three plump wood pigeons nesting in clumps of green succulent nettles. We found no trees on the island. Only a few elm shrubs stunted and lacerated by the winds.

As we trampled down an area of bracken to give space for a picnic lunch I thanked God that this wasn't virgin Africa or India. St. Patrick, bless him, certainly had done a decent job – not a snake in sight!

Plans started formulating in my head. They remained silent. Shirley almost reading my mind remarked,

"There is a lot of hard work ahead of us".

I agreed. We savoured the ambience, the moment. The sentinel gulls eyed us suspiciously but refused to leave their perches. Their nests would be on the ground somewhere around the homestead or haggard[3] area. No need to disturb them right now.

My years in Africa had taught me much. Most of all when in the bush – and this certainly was – keep still, watch and wonder. One will be amazed. I thought of that dark continent as we climbed to the highest cairn that afternoon and surveyed all about us.

For over yonder to the east and nestling within Ballyhealy Bay was the reason I took off for East Africa in 1952. There lay the romantic and scenic farm of the Ryan family, Ballytrent. I pointed the binoculars to a clump of trees, probably about six miles away across the bay, and asked Shirley to take a look.

"What am I looking at or for?"

"There lies the reason for my taking off to East Africa in 1952. That's Ballytrent, the home farm of Jim Ryan. The man who offered me my first job."

His farm, Ballyvistea, far off in Molo amongst the White Highlands of Kenya Colony was an enormous mixed farm of corn crops, sheep, cattle, pigs, horses and pyrethrum.

---

[3] Descriptive area enveloping farm homestead buildings in Ireland.

A PINCH OF SALTEE

I had never asked myself why I did take off. Everyone of my age seemed, in the early fifties, to be doing just that. Finish Uni and vanish. I followed suit.

The boat trip on the British India 'Kenya', the first steps on Mombasa's filthy stifling streets, the smells – spices, rotting fruit, open sewerage - the potholes, casual dress, but most of all, the climate enraptured me with a desire to remain and fulfil. It was all terribly exotic to a young fairly naïve Irishman.

I fell in love with Africa. That affair lasted forty years.

Having learnt to understand the vagaries of snakes, scorpions and the like I was now smug and confident as I walked through this islands undergrowth in shorts and sandals. I was back in Ireland and not a worry in sight of beasties that go bump in the night!

My imagination, always an active volcano, was at that moment near eruption. Plans to re-establish the farm, the buildings, restock and replant, foster the endangered seabird species. All these and more flashed vividly across my wide screen of thought which took up most of my waking hours. I had never been one for dreams, that is night time dreams, but right now a few kaleidoscopic ideas did intrude into my normally passive sleeping periods. One such item was having a mechanical hoist to lift things from the mooring to nearby our homestead. I could see it so clearly, operated by a small Briggs and Stratton engine, with loads of baggage swinging from the wire like a Swiss ski lift. "Dream on", I would say to myself! It would, however, make life a lot easier I predicted.

I had found out at an early age that I was a child of the soil. Born into the farming estate life of East Galway with horses, cattle, sheep and pigs as the main course it was hunting, shooting and fishing that created the recipe for dessert. Having attended Prep school at St. Gerards, Bray, Co. Wicklow and public school at Ampleforth College, Yorkshire, England, an agricultural based future seemed on the cards. In this I followed the footsteps of my cousin John Bland (JB), a couple of years senior to me, by attending Plasnewydd Training and Dairy Farm outside Denbigh in North Wales. I had obtained entrances to both Reading University and Cirencester Agricultural College. JB, after his year of practical dairying went on to the University of North Wales, Bangor, and thence to the family estate in County Laois. I didn't have a farm to return to. A vivid premonition in 1939 made my father pessimistic about his return from the approaching war. I had overheard my father and mother talking after breakfast one day. He was complaining about not sleeping well and having to put up with a recurring nightmare. He said "he could see himself in ragged uniform drifting in a life raft in an unfriendly ocean. He was very sick and feared starvation." It never allowed him to witness the ending but his fear of 'lost at sea' was wholly prominent. 'This was most bizzare' he said as he was an infantry man. He was colonel of the Rifle Brigade, the 60th. Therefore why should he ever be in a life raft?

He duly sold our Mountbellew estate and moved my mother, sister and myself to Ballyboughal in North County Dublin. Our beloved ponies, Fergus and Freckles, accompanied us. He was almost right. He did see out the war years, his Second World War, but succumbed to cancer in 1947 after a heroic battle. I was very close to him. Much more so than to my mother. I, without knowing at the time, suffered an immense loss. I was left rudderless – I had to make my own way. I became very independent at an early age.

My practical year at Plasnewydd now completed I was competing at the 1952 RDS Horse Show when I was high jacked off my horses back. I was made an offer, I just couldn't refuse, especially at that age. No more studying, off to Africa with me. On consulting my mother who, unknown to me, had already been briefed by John Ryan (Jim's brother) on the African offer replied:

"It's your life, darling. Make up your own mind."

A PINCH OF SALTEE

Within a month I had packed my bags, kissed my mother goodbye and hugged, with lasting endearment, my beloved nanny of thirteen years, Nan Nolan. Tears welled in her already bloodshot eyes. I flew to London. There I met up with Jim's general manager, Harold Madderson, a bronzed New Zealander, with the flattest accent I had ever heard, who was returning from overseas leave with his family. I sailed away into the sun to a life unplanned, unknown. Harold, on our second day afloat, presented me with a little green book entitled 'Up Country Swahili'.

"Read it, inwardly digest it and at each breakfast I will expect you to know ten new words. Ok?"

I remember I was dumbfounded. Rooted to the deck. Back at school I thought when all I wanted was to enjoy games, swimming and meeting new people for the next three weeks. I did what I was told. I amazed myself and all the others at our table. But what a wise move it had been. No African on the farm could speak a word of English!

My love for the soil and things earthy grew and grew. I dressed in shorts and open-necked short sleeved shirts. My body responded like a Barberton daisy to the warmth of the sun. It made me feel so well within myself.

My first five years in Africa were made up of two in farming, three in armed conflict in the battle to conquer the Mau Mau revolt. Protagonists of this revolution, to oust the 'white man' in Kenya came mainly from the countries most populous tribe, the Kikuyu. Their leader, Jomo Kenyata, had graduated from Moscow University and the London School of Economics. He was thought to be a rabid communist. The cult employed fear tactics to initiate tribes folk into their organisation. They also instilled terror into their intended white victims by stringing up dead cats on their farm gateposts. This was a warning. The hamstringing of their cattle was tantamount to 'leave now or else'. They wanted UHURU, freedom.

Kenyata was put in prison at Kapenguria, Northern Province, for many years by the Colonial administration for alleged subversion and plotting against the State. He had the last laugh, however, when he was elected his country's first president in 1963. His tenure was probably the most enlightened governorship of any African country since independence. He proved to be an excellent leader and father figure for many years.

All able bodied people, male and female, were called up or volunteered for various segments of the armed forces.

Jim had five managers on the farm and advised three of us to 'get in at the start and return to me quickly'. Our positions would be kept open.

Those three years played a most significant factor in the decades that followed. My nerves were shattered at the end of that period of active service. Massacres, ambushes, close quarter combat, near misses and the 'killing of people' factor kept reappearing in nightmarish episodes for at least six years.

Probably my most frightening episode was the first time I was ambushed. My patrol - one other officer, David Andrews, and five African Askaris[4] - was following up the trail of a gang who had hamstrung a dozen cattle on a farm on the Kinankop where our group of reservists were stationed with 39 Brigade. This was a fertile area on the west of the Aberdare Mountains. Gangs of Mau Mau would invade, undercover of darkness, hamstring as many cattle as possible and drive off the rest of the herd. They would make for the thickly forested slopes of the Aberdares and be well up into them by first light. Some cattle would then be slaughtered and distributed to the gang with some meat buried for future consumption.

The gang would then be well fed and rested up by the time we, the patrols, were trucked to the farm to start the 'follow up' operation. Our African Askari trackers would then set off, as bloodhounds would, following the gang's trail. They – two of

---

[4] Soldiers/policemen

them – were armed with pangas[5] only, allowing them ease and speed of movement. We had to keep up with these fleet footed bush craftsmen and also keep an alert eye out for anything untoward. A very tiring and stressful task.

Any enemy operating in his or her own environment is a way better than someone out of their patch. We were, therefore, usually onto a hiding to nothing. Vigilance and that extra sense came very much into play.

We would be carrying a pack with provisions for a maximum of seventy-two hours. David and I were armed with 3x36 Grenades each, a point 45 revolver and the latest British submachine gun, the Patchett. This was 1953. The Askaris had Lee Enfield .303 rifles.

It might take hours to get close to, or even catch up with, the gang who anyway might well have split up after their meal and rest.

Dogged might well describe us. Intrepid, foolish, might also work. We had a mission – seek, encounter, destroy. This was our task, our duty.

We had just left the cover of the bamboo forest at approximately ten thousand feet above sea level when we came under rapid fire from our left flank. We were in a glade and tall elephant grass covered most of the area. There was an overpowering smell of rotting manure.

I immediately sank to the ground with David behind me. I looked left, he right. We didn't return the fire.

Once I had counted my unit and seen that all were unharmed I made a plan. David and two Askaris should 'leopard crawl' through the grass to the left of where we had heard the firing. I would take the rest straight ahead. We would crawl for as long as possible or until the enemy opened fire a second time. This we wanted to happen anyway in order to locate them.

---

[5] Knives - Machetes

A PINCH OF SALTEE

Our plan then was to charge with all guns blazing. Our two trackers would move out to the right flank and be ready for armed combat if needs be or follow any of the enemy who escaped our onslaught.

It was very much a game of cat and mouse. Who would make the first move and from where. Nothing stirred – for an age.

I decided to attack. I waved a signal to David and his team. We raced forward, crouching, guns at the ready.

A single shot rang out just to my left and ahead of us – a second came from a little to the right. I heard the zing of the bullets as they fortunately flew overhead. That meant the enemy were literally fifty metres straight in front of us by my reckoning.

We broke cover and fired from the hip, spraying 9mm bullets in a slight arc left and right of us.

One further single shot – now from the forest ahead of us – a random shot, I hoped, in retreat maybe?

It was a case of them or us and we wanted them.

I saw shadows fleeing through the dim lit forest. My Patchett was trained on them for brief and spasmodic bursts.

Next thing I heard was cries from my Askaris – they had found two dead bodies and one wounded one. I called off the attack. My trackers were loath to this but discipline won out.

On reflection those bodies could have been ours. That time it was us who were more deadly and accurate. We had the better fire power.

I learnt then that I didn't think of my own safety. I just went in and at'em. Maybe I had seen too many John Wayne movies?

I slept with my eyes open a lot at that time. It is possible believe me! That was an unsettling juncture in my life. I didn't seem to be able to concentrate on one thing for any reasonable period. Hence, after leaving Kenya a rather rolling stone attitude to life had me cattle ranching, repping[6] (liquor agencies) followed

---

[6] Selling

9

by five years of radio and television presenting in Rhodesia. All along, however, I kept the blood knot for farming ever present with a small holding of my own outside Bulawayo, Southern Rhodesia.[7] On this I trained race horses, with some success, and fattened cattle.

Kenya had taught me just how much the human body could be put through and withstand. I had somehow become a workaholic. Hours of intense labour, with sometimes two or three different jobs at one time being common placed. These never worried me, especially as I have always had the highest of high objectives for getting things done 'now' and as perfect as possible. On reflection I must have been hell to live with in those years. Our family crest bears the motto 'tout en haut' – all from above. This perhaps was why I have always been a fatalist. Fate having played such a major role throughout my life.

During the next three decades I made a habit of returning every four years or so to Ireland. Never once did I neglect to visit the island. They were rapid trips but plans for an eventual future project were ever rampant in my mind.

Finally with retirement due after the completion of our Indian sojourn Shirley and I visited Kilmore Quay on a fact finding mission. It was a two hour drive from our house in Dublin so firstly we looked for, and found, a well situated B & B. We were fortunate. We found an even more wonderful family who owned it. Greg and Philomena Stafford also ran a large dairy farm with their son, Rory. They also had three thoroughbred mares with foals and had a couple of horses in training with Aidan O'Brien. This was a feather in his cap as Aidan was one of Ireland's leading race horse trainers dealing primarily with millionaires and only taking on the 'best horses'. We found we had much in common.

---

[7] Now Zimbabee

A PINCH OF SALTEE

They had a great interest in the islands which could be viewed from anywhere on their farm.

Stafford is a household name in County Wexford Their home and farm soon became our second home, our office, warehouse and holding ground for livestock. What a jewel in the crown as Kilmore Quay in itself is a treasure trove of unheralded beauty. Riches culinary, human, marine, residential all abound. And virtually untouched by mass housing development. Thatched cottages to the left, thatched houses to the right.

Next on our list, putting our preferences in the correct order, would be the culinary and beverage outlets. Here we were overly impressed with the Silver Fox Restaurant, situated in a bungalow-style residence opposite the Kilmore Quay lifeboat house and just 100m from the pier.

Kehoe's Pub, on the main street down to the Quay and opposite the Catholic Church, was an eye opener. Set up by James Kehoe, a Dublin actuary and stalwart helmsman whose thatched house adjoins, the pub is a maritime museum. Superb historical artefacts, memorabilia, prints, paintings and cartography fill the walls and ceilings of a constantly crowded establishment.

A little further down the street and much nearer the Quay is the elder statesman of the village, the Wooden House. This watering hole goes back to the 1890's and is also steeped in maritime history. It had recently been purchased by a Dublin business man builder, Cormac McCarthy, who outlined his future plans and ideas to us. Kilmore Quay would have a brand new and revamped hostelry within a few years.

At the entrance to the village and almost opposite the Garda Station is the Saltees Hotel run by the Byrne brothers. This had fourteen bedrooms, a lounge bar, restaurant and disco/dance hall. A hub for wedding receptions.

Kilmore Quay therefore seemed to be well served by these outlets which together with a half dozen B & B's catered for the summer influx of tourists. After all this was the sunny south-east!

A PINCH OF SALTEE

Warmer than anywhere else in the country with more sun hours. Or so the blurb said?

Kehoe is another well recognised Wexford name. Already mentioned is the pub but then we found it on the hardware store. Primarily a ship's chandlers, it was the only provider of such goods in the district, but also had most items for D.I.Y. and builders. It was next door to the lifeboat house.

Coxswain of this famous lifeboat, the Mary Margaret, was Johnny Devereux. Here it is pronounced with the emphasis on the 'X' and not as I did, the French style without the 'X'! I was politely put right by this kindly warm personage, Johnny. I had remembered the name from my childhood days and associated it with another gentle, soft-spoken man who took people out and around the islands. Bates and Devereux were the two doyen fishing families of the Quay. Their elders had passed on to their respective 'great fishing grounds in the sky' whilst the next generations were still plying their trade in things maritime.

Johnny had a thirty foot fishing boat – Celtic Lady – which he used for taking out eight/ten fishermen on day trips. He combined this with his voluntary role as Cox of the RNLI boat. It was his father, Jack, I had remembered all those long years ago. I loved the angle of Johnny's well-worn but faded blue captain's cap. Slightly tilted down over his right eye it somehow emphasised the genuine twinkle in his eyes.

"Are you the same man that's mentioned as the owner of the island in the book?" he gently quizzed me.

"Well not quite the same man, he was my grandfather", I answered.

"So are you going to resettle, so to speak, the island after all these years?"

"Yes, I suppose you could say we are."

"Well, good luck to you. If there is anything I can assist you with don't hesitate to call me. Are you getting a boat by the way?"

"Oh definitely yes", I replied. "In time".

A PINCH OF SALTEE

With that he touched his cap and bade us farewell.

The book referred to by Johnny was 'Saltees: Islands of Birds and Legends' by Richard Roche and Oscar Merne. A well researched historical archive of the islands which I had travelled with since the late seventies when first published.

Kilmore Quay also has a small supermarket, a couple of other general stores, a post office and 'chipper' so the residents of the village seemed well provided for. Two fish factories and a fish cooperative employed over one hundred locals, mostly women. This then was the village and community we were to become part of. That evening we checked into Mill Road bed and breakfast. After being shown to our room, Saltees, overlooking the bay and islands, I went out with Greg to see their farm. Shirley remained in the room to have an early shower and do some reading on the local district from journals and brochures provided by Philomena.

Born and bred a farmer Greg said he was never out of flat cap and wellies unless Philomena banned him from the house as 'too mucky'. Both of them had farmed the land and milked the herd for twenty years before they agreed for Rory to gradually take over the responsibilities and manual work. Phil then found herself without enough to do. She talked Greg into building onto and refurbishing their farmhouse so that she could run a tidy little bed and breakfast business. Their warmth and personalities were infectious. One couldn't help but like them. Mill Road became the hub of our activity within the area from that day onwards.

Perhaps, as both Shirley and I were equestrians and as a lot of the recent talk with Greg was about horses we appreciated our challenge ahead. Rather like getting ready for the La Touche Cup at Punchestown. A race with the widest variety of obstacles imaginable and competed for over a formidable four and a quarter miles. And a race I had won in the mid eighties. Something similar was obviously ahead of us. Were we up to it?

A PINCH OF SALTEE

Chapter Two

Shirley – Oscar – Opening up the Island –
The Buildings – Declan

On returning from Kenya in the early 1990's I found myself at a total loss of what to do. It had to be something active so to occupy my immediate needs I returned to my favourite pastime the training of race horses.

The small training establishment I leased was near Ashbourne, north County Dublin. I intended point-to-pointing and hopefully then sell them on as potential steeplechasers. This was something I had done successfully and profitably on my last stay back in the early eighties.

A friend from schooldays, the elder brother of one of my best pals at SHAC[8] and I used to party together in the holidays, invited me over for drinks and supper. He had heard I was in the neighbourhood. This was to be another historic day. Another dream was to come true.

Jamie was one of those old school colonial Irish types, who went abroad for most of his life, made a tidy sum, had tried a couple of wives but never got to the finish line. He was now living the life of Riley, on his own, in a divine Queen Ann home near Ballyboughal. Although quite a lot older than me we had kept in touch down the years.

His visitors that night were four ladies and one gentleman none of whom I knew. They were the huntin' shootin' country set alright but a little beyond their competitive years. That was the evening I met Shirley.

Jamie's kitchen was old fashioned – Aga cooker, quarry tiles, copper utensils hanging from walls and a massive 'clean washed' old pine table as centre piece. His delft was Dutch blue, his cutlery old Irish silver. But there was no formality. Jamie had

---

[8] Senior Houses Ampleforth College

14

A PINCH OF SALTEE

a housekeeper who laid everything on before departing and cleaned it all up in the morning.

The seven of us hit it off as right from the start, the mood was electric. We moved from a roaring log fire in his sitting room to the kitchen, each caressing a fine piece of Waterford in well warmed hands. I asked Shirley if she minded me carrying her glass through.

"I'm going to grab a seat near the Aga. Would you mind sitting near the warmth?" "No, go ahead. I'll sit wherever you would like me to". I had noticed she wasn't as exuberant as the others and had obviously accompanied one of the ladies to the party. She hadn't met Jamie before. She seemed a little lost.

Over supper I noticed she wasn't keen on the casserole that was served as a main course and when asked the reason she quietly told me she was almost vegetarian. I put that right by offering to get her a second helping of the smoked salmon we had as a starter.

"Please don't bother or make a fuss. I'm fine with vegetables alone" she replied. She touched my arm quite tenderly and then in attempting to stop me from rising held it quite firmly. I automatically closed my hand on hers and caressed it lightly. Our eyes met. Mine transmitted 'trust me, its fine'.

Once she realised it was no trouble, that no one really cared or even looked at her questioningly, she relaxed.

Shirley had been a widow for eight years and had four children spread around the world. Two daughters, one in India, one in USA and two sons, one in Canada and the other in Dublin. She had been interested in horses from childhood and had ridden competitively 'till she started to produce her family. But she had taken it up again in later life and especially since her husband's death. She was a Wicklow lady. Her father had been a stockbroker in Dublin but relaxed on the back of a horse, preferably out hunting and point-to-pointing. She inherited all his equestrian desires.

I invited her to visit my stables and ride out with me. She took up the offer some days later. I was a little perturbed by

A PINCH OF SALTEE

Shirley's height. She was pretty as a rose, lithe and lean. At 5ft. 10ins., however, she was tall for exercise riding. On my morning workouts she would have to sit much shorter than she had ever done before. My strategy was to allow her to ride long – like show jumping style – for the first few mornings. Then she had to pull up her stirrups at least four holes[9]. I didn't wish my 'pilot' to feel unhappy, unstable, and unsure atop my two novices. Neither of them had run in a hurdle or steeplechase but Shirley could certainly school them over small fences at the start. I was too heavy to jump them at speed. Bad for their legs.

As it turned out Shirley took to work riding and short stirrups like a boot to a good leg. She had hunted with the Bray Harriers from childhood progressing to riding 'between the flags' as point-to-points were called. This was a dangerous sport in those days as racing took place over open country including ploughed fields, ditches, rivers, hedges and banks. All races were over three miles. Once her children had made their ways into the outside world Shirley returned to leisure riding and took part in dressage, her favourite discipline. We were about the same age I surmised. We were both free spirits and loved a lot of the same things.

Over the next four months we found we had much in common. Horses, dogs, walking, tennis, golf, reading, movies and theatre. The only thing we did not have in common was sailing. Shirley and her late husband had been intrepid yachtsmen, cruising and competing. They were also members of the Royal St. George Yacht Club, Dublin. Her son Tony, also a member of the RSt.GYC had followed their footsteps and was also a very competitive sailor.

Luck ran out on me during the next four months. Firstly one of my mares got badly cut by a sharp stone which was unearthed whilst galloping early one morning. I was told by my vet that it would take a long time to heal. Then my second horse pulled a tendon. This meant that racing was out of the question.

---

[9] 4 inches approximately

A PINCH OF SALTEE

My dream of having another winner vanished into thin air. Perhaps, however, fate was on hand. Another winner might well have joined me!

We visited Shirley's daughter, Vicki, in India some months later. We remained there for over two years. I hasten to add not with her daughter all the time. We were invited to set up an equestrian centre and run an organic mixed farm outside Bangalore. It was during those hectic years that our love and friendship grew to form an unstoppable team.

On our return to Dublin, Shirley invited me to move into her home. I had no need to stay on in north County Dublin without any horses. Also it was too far to be travelling back and forward to be with each other. I invited Shirley to join me in the island project. We agreed to both requests.

Oscar came into our life like the first ray of summer on a field of sunflowers. Each flower craning its neck, hopefully extracting all warmth from the daily visitation of that sunny character. Little did we know, one overcast Wednesday morning, we were to find a new member of our family. We set out from home to collect Shirley's sister, Patricia, at Ashford, Co. Wicklow for our weekly walk with her and her dog Berry.

The well kept complex set high in the hills close to Rathdrum, County Wicklow, boasted forty odd and colourful residents when we drove into its yard. We didn't really know what to expect, rather like the first day at boarding school. Would they be noisy and exuberant or meek and shy? Would we instantly gel or would it be a gradual process of meeting, conversing and "getting to know you" like Anna and her children in Siam? Those children were all different. So were these dear hearts – very different. This was the County Wicklow pound and we had come to look for a lovely dog in less fortunate circumstances. We have always had dogs and horses but since returning from India we had a void in our lives. We needed to fill that space.

A PINCH OF SALTEE

The main building is constructed in a cartwheel design with twenty or so separate kennels and runs. Here we viewed every breed that is known and some that would be hard to categorise. We fell in love with Henry, an enormous mastiff type with big anxious eyes, smooth black coat and a short tail. There was an instant rapport.

"Too big. Imagine him in our house. He's gorgeous but 'no'" was Shirley's firm comment.

"He could be a fighter", chipped in Patricia.

"I like him", said I "but I agree he's too big".

There was nothing else that took our fancy until I spied a gorgeous lemon and white Springer Spaniel in an adjoining compound.

"That would be perfect", both Shirley and I blurted out on sighting it.

We went over to have a close look but were cut short in our tracks,

"Sorry, but that one's taken", said the lady warden.

It was a male, about a year old and in very good condition.

"Pity about that", I casually expressed my sorrow.

"You wouldn't by any chance have another such hidden away would you", I questioned the lady.

"Take a look in that shed over there", she replied pointing to an old style hay barn now completely closed in with only one visible door.

Neatly constructed parallel pens ran away from a central passage. Once again a cornucopia of canine intensity greeted my stares. These were much noisier than the others we had viewed. They ran up and down the mesh dividers, jumping, skipping, yowling and howling. Tails were a-wagging "plenty to the dozen". The blending of Jeyes and canine odours wafted hygienically throughout the shed.

Nothing immediately caught my eye but then as I was almost at the end of the barn a little head, liver and white in colour, with long hanging ears and tearful eyes peeped out from a kennel at the rear of the last pen. Three other dogs, much bigger, were already actively engaged in attempting to attract my attention in that same pen. I was drawn to this little mite with the doleful look. It tentatively moved out of its kennel, it was tiny.

"What's that"? I said to the warden with obvious joy in my voice.

"He is twelve weeks old, a registered Springer Spaniel and he's a dote. Let me catch and bring him to you".

As she handed this little, now highly energised, bundle of mirth to me, I drew him close to my chest and smelt that very special puppy odour. He licked and licked and licked that sensitive spot beneath my chin wriggling all the time. Quiet gurgles erupted between licks. They, I am sure, translated into "please hold me tight, tight. Please take me me me with you". I heard those plaintive requests as I carried him out into the sunlight. Shirley and Patricia saw me coming; they erupted into smiles and laughter. I let the puppy down onto the ground. That was the first time any of us had seen him free and in entirety.

He was a robust bundle of energy with an enormous extended tummy. Beautiful marking of liver red on white defined the outlines of his face and ears. A marked white pathway stretched from nose to between his eyes then ears to join his almost white but speckled body. Just above his tail was a large red spot. He had enormous paws.

He stayed close to my feet as I walked across to the ladies. His ears were actively employed as he noticed things along his way.

Shirley fell for him immediately. She too picked him up and got washed with exuberant kisses.

A couple of hours later, after our walk at Avondale, we returned to the pound with a paid up dog licence obtained in Rathdrum. We had eaten a sandwich lunch outside a local pub and discussed the new addition at length. I handed over proof of licence to the warden together with a donation for the ongoing welfare of the place.

A PINCH OF SALTEE

"By the way", she said "his name is Kerry".

Somehow, we didn't like the name but decided on our drive back to take time over a new one. He slept all the way and didn't get car sick. A great bonus!

At 3.15am next morning Shirley woke me and said "Oscar, that's his name". I liked it. I agreed and went back to sleep. From then on that little dote grew into something - someone – very special. Oscar became a member of our family. He travelled almost everywhere with us. He was to play a major part, less than a year later, when I ran into a medical nightmare.

Next purchase we made for the island was a Honda strimmer – the commercial size, a little bigger and stronger than the regular garden one. This was essential as we had to cut paths through the bracken to make it easier for ourselves and anyone else who visited. Like Oscar!

From our landing place on the western shore there was a pathway honed out between two undulations rising up to the homestead. Occasional flat stones were becoming evident along this route as we firstly hacked and then strimmed a way through. The original paved pathway was being unearthed. I started strimming but within a year this duty was taken over completely by Shirley who told everybody "she absolutely adored the task. I find I transfer myself into another world. I am set a task to clean up the place – it could be the world – and I'm allowed to get on with it. It's up to me to do a good job. And what a joy to look back, at the end of a day, at what I've achieved. Something visible, tangible, that is going to have a useful purpose."

That first autumn we strimmed and then cleared all the bracken and brambles from inside and around the homestead area. With no animal movement during the best part of the last half century, save for rabbit runs, weeds and bracken had progressively advanced over most of the land. We then strimmed around the nearest and what looked like the deepest waterhole. This we measured by striding over the land in the straightest line. It was close to six hundred metres east of the homestead. Shirley set about clearing off the watercress and other alien weeds. We unearthed an old, very old, cooking pot, kettle and a couple of horse shoes. The waterhole was circular in shape, about five metres across with two run-offs which, in the depth of winter, would have taken a fair amount of overflow cascading down a ten metre drop to the rocks below, one of many waterfalls on the eastern side that Declan and other fishermen had told us about.. I immediately named it 'Shirley's' as she was already fashioning a mini dam wall and closing off the other overflow path. She had taken charge of its renovation.

My time in Africa had taught me to conserve water at every possible place at every possible time. Nothing is more essential than H2O. In India we found it similarly necessary to conserve. Monsoons may come and go with due regularity but drought appears roughly every seven years and that means devastation. We didn't have to discuss conservation at length, we just worked at it as a matter of course. Mental telepathy is a marvellous medium when you are a team.

Each time we visited the island we would check the pastures, waterholes and then the birds before starting any manual work. The Saltees are bird sanctuaries with over one hundred species visible at different times of the year. Certain endangered species like Manx Shearwater and Puffin nest on ours. These above all else had to be protected.

With general ecological matters on my mind I invited Eugene Wallace of the Wild Life Department to pay us a visit. He lived locally and was a regular visitor to the big island.

A small intense man, he strode over the entire acreage pointing out this, explaining that, and stopping every so often to examine a recent nest. Here he showed us the different bone remains, explaining the feeding habits of the different species.

We have a quite famous colony of Cormorants breeding on the island. Their cousins the Shags are also residents. Eugene explained to us that over the decades of non farming and therefore no stocking of animals the Cormorants had taken over a number of the stone walls as their nesting grounds. We had already witnessed this earlier in the year. I noted it was only walls on the eastern side of the island. That acrid aroma of rotting fish seemed heavily engrained in each nook and cranny of those forgotten walls.

He showed us the burrows used by Shearwaters to nest in and similar holes near the cliff edges where Puffins nested. A lot of Fulmars patrolled the shorelines. I remarked how they reminded me of the old hurricane fighters of the Second World War. So chunky but graceful in flight. Eugene agreed.

On returning to the homestead for lunch and whilst Shirley was preparing it Eugene and I went 'walk-about' in the immediate area. He was a fund of knowledge pointing out the various granary items used down the centuries.

"Those large mounds so beautifully faced in stone were used for drying the grain crops", he said "and notice the over hanging stones – that was to prevent any vermin climbing up the face. You should restore them when you get time" he finished with as he strode to an outcrop of metal peeping through a bunch of tall nettles.

"That's the hub. A horse used to walk around in a circle here with a harness onto a spindle turning that cogged wheel. From there a drive shaft ran back into that house onto a grinding machine. You remember, don't you?" He winked at me with a smug smile on his rugged face.

"They would feed the bags of whole grain into the machine and out the other end would come rolled oats, barley, etc. Pierces of Wexford would have made the machinery I bet".

All the time he was bent double looking for further evidence of what went on here in those long lost times.

"Are you going to restore this by any chance?"

"No, not likely. The buildings yes, but I don't see us having any crops. That will be for the next generation to decide" I replied as I guided him back to the haggard and lunch.

A PINCH OF SALTEE

Over a scrumptious cold salad picnic, Eugene expressed his thoughts about the buildings.

"They were designed around a format used four and five centuries ago and maybe even older than that", he said. "That end room there would have been where they boiled the feed for the stock during the winter. It would also, most probably, have been used as the farrier's workshop. You know, all iron work. You will probably find old horse shoes, tynes, nuts, bolts and the like. They will come to light all over the place. You'll have great fun if you use a metal detector! All along there," still pointing to the west side, "would have been the cow sheds and horse stalls. They probably all have cobbled stone floors with good drainage. The two end houses would be for grain stores. That side over there," now pointing to the east, "was probably for housing the smaller stock – pigs, sheep and poultry and the like. Have you found the well yet? It will be around here somewhere"

I managed to finally get a word in with a negative reply about the well.

As we landed back at Kilmore Quay, Eugene thanked Shirley profusely for her hospitality and good meal:

"And Henry, I will be sending you some thoughts on conserving the birds. Thanks a lot both of you. I hope you will invite me again".

Back on the island a vivid emerald ocean of bracken spread out in front of me as I battled through its immense growth. It was my first attempt at quantifying the extent of pasture to non-pasture areas. Single taller fronds of fern reached up like arms waving to a t.v. camera in a crowd scene.

Some grand pieces of pasture, now in full growth with stems lush green, lengthy and simply longing to be guzzled up by some four legged lovelies, were evident. They definitely would provide enough fodder, initially at any rate, for a small number of stock. Archival research had shown me that the brilliant little native Kerry cattle, together with the British Shorthorn had been farmed on both islands.

I consulted cousin John (JB) who had now retired from the day to day farming of his estate having handed Blandsfort over to his two sons, David and Peter. He, however, was now even more active in agriculture – but this time in the government departments new R.E.P.S. (Rural Environmental Protection Scheme) programme. He was an official 'planner' so I consulted him. He was confident that the island would qualify for funding under the scheme. He would check that we were part of a Natural Heritage Area (NHA) and a Special Area of Conservation (SAC). These are areas of special interest to the E.U. as they contain habitats, species, fauna and flora which all need to be conserved. For this, funding from Europe is available. Good farming practice and husbandry may continue arm-in-arm within these areas. The deterioration of habitats and disturbance of species must be avoided. In County Wexford alone there are forty-one such recognised SAC's.

After visiting the island J.B. and I settled down into a snug at Kehoe's Pub to an intense brainstorming session. To control the bracken, we agreed, I should stock with both sheep and cattle. There seemed to be ample water with at least half the island providing good grazing.

Greg Stafford had told me that he had heard, a long time ago, from a fellow who had grazed the vacant island with sheep that there was a great growth of late autumn grass which 'held them over the winter'. I proffered this snippet of nutritional nuance for what it was worth. A plan was evolving. J.B. went away to do some sums and put an actual feasibility study into operation.

I knew I was jumping the gun a bit but already I could see a flock of Connemara hornies – they are the toughest and shaggiest sheep breed in Ireland – and if they could survive the rigours of the western mountain ranges and shorelines they assuredly could survive the Saltees.

A PINCH OF SALTEE

It was easy to dream about flocks and herds but little did I realise the logistical and mechanical equation I was setting myself. Was this perhaps called a headache? First things first, however, I cautioned myself. Shirley and I discussed a budget. How much could I afford to spend annually on this project? Was it only a dream or was it feasible? Would I be able to work the land like it had been worked all those years ago? Half a century had flown by since any husbandry of fauna or flora had taken place.

Were we, at our stage of life, septuagenarians asking too much of ourselves? I am an all time optimist. Shirley is not. The perfect combination perchance. My drive to see a project to finality had always been supercharged. A titan in my endeavours with an indestructible belief in my own ability. Many times, however, I have come up short. Somehow the Saltee situation seemed supremely satisfying and attainable. Shirley showed willing.

All these ideas were becoming a mite questionable so I needed answers and quickly.

"Who better than Declan", I suggested, "to tell us what boats are available and how we should plan our trips over the next few months".

"Absolutely right, so lets get him into Kehoes and pick his brains", was Shirley's instant reply. That was as easy as done. There was no prompting Declan when a pint or three was on offer.

My first impression of Declan Bates had not been one of warmth and friendship. A little distant and cautious I thought. Perhaps a little sceptical of us and our plans. I got the feeling that he 'had boat, would travel' and that was that. No time for small talk and not a bit keen on giving out information of any kind. He was obviously a wealthy man with three trawlers, a large pleasure boat, the 'Saltees Princess' and Tapaidh on which we had been ferried a number of times already.

Eden, his house overlooking the bay and islands, next to the post office at the village end of a scenic piece of real estate was also a valuable and well appointed asset.

A PINCH OF SALTEE

Shirley and I decided on an early supper at Kehoes. We liked to get in before the rush. After all this was mid summer 1998. Tourists were everywhere.

Declan joined us at 9.00pm. He immediately had the first of a few pints of Heineken. We discussed at length our plans for the island. He offered us the use (not free of course) of his metal barge. A 30 ft. open boat which could be used for transporting anything, i.e. sheep, cattle, timber, building products. He would tow it behind Tapaidh and we could pole it in the last hundred metres or so he explained.

"It'll have to be done on an incoming tide, you'll appreciate. Otherwise it will get stranded and I wouldn't want to wait there twelve hours you know. You'll have to be quick with the unloading. My time is precious".

We agreed with all he said. We had to. We had no alternative. The meeting, however, was cordial and good humoured. I thought we were actually warming to each other. In my opinion he had thawed a lot.

"A man very much interested in his bank account", I remarked to Shirley as we walked to our car, parked, as were all the other patron's, in the Church car park opposite.

At breakfast next morning Philomena remarked on our meeting with Declan and asked,

"How did you get on with him?"

"Oh, well enough" we replied in unison as she departed with our order.

"News travels fast in this village", I smiled across at Shirley.

On returning with our twin piled plates of FIB's (full Irish breakfasts), Phil opened the floodgates of innuendo. It wasn't so much the quantity of content but the quality that counted.

"Declan very much thinks he's top seadog down on the quay you know. He has the sole rights on trips to the islands.

Whatever he says goes. You wouldn't want to get on the wrong side of him, I tell you, for what its worth".

"Have you enough toast there. Do you need another pot of tea. You know he's very cosy with the Neales of the big island, don't you? Enjoy your meal," and she departed to the kitchen.

We were down ahead of the other three couples so we pondered her remarks over the remainder of our meal. It was obvious we had to cooperate in every which way. We needed his assistance. It would be on his terms. This didn't worry me a bit for if he offered the best service then I would demand 'the best service'. And hopefully get it.

Declan was all smiles as we met up on the pier at eleven o'clock. His smiles, however, were not solely for us. He had a full boat load of ten other passengers.

"I'll drop you off on the way back from the big island as I don't wish to delay them, you know", he said as he closed the iron chain across the entrance to the boat.

"That'll do us just fine. What time will you return for all of us then?" I enquired as he got behind the wheel and reversed Tapaidh out of the marina.

"Will four o'clock be time enough for you?"

"Yes indeed and thanks a million," was my reply.

Shirley had got talking to two Americans entwined with telescopes, cameras and goodness knows what else. I stayed a little distance away looking at the course Declan was taking to the big island. I couldn't help but over hear the remarkable high pitched New York twang which cut through the roar of Tapaidh's turbines.

"Oh my god you actually plan to live out there – on your own, without electricity!!"

'Yes, America,' I thought. 'Where now is your pioneering instinct? What would they ever do without McDonalds?'

To land on the big island passengers had to embark onto a small punt of Declan's which was permanently moored one hundred metres offshore. Declan gunned the little six horse power

27

outboard into action and ferried them to the slipway. There is no pier or jetty. It must have been difficult enough building the little strip of concrete onto which everyone landed.

Our island doesn't even boast that luxury. The same principle of landing applies but dependant on where the tide is we are deposited either onto slippery, kelp coated rocks or into two feet of water. From there we have to tread very, very carefully up, along and over mountains of boulders, rocks, shale and sometimes a little sandy beach. It's not easy and its made much more difficult and dangerous if one is carrying anything.

Today we just had a picnic cooler box, camera, briefcase containing measuring tape, recorder, radio and an A4 tablet of paper for copious notations and sketches.

It was yet another lovely day. Wispy curls of cloud painted ever changing images on a bright blue backdrop. The ocean had an azure sheen about it. It must have been almost low tide as the defining line of St. Patrick's Bridge was most evident. Flat calm to the east, slight ripples on the west. Fresh iodinic aromas jostled ones nasal cavities vying for precedence. Bird life was abundant, so were bunnies. They skuttered away from the alien sounds of our movement. Young gulls, some about to break out of their shells, others, spotted bundles of fluff, were hobbling about and 'cheeping' endlessly that sonorous note of 'food, food, food'.

We had decided to give the buildings a thorough look over on this visit. Remember that they had last been occupied in 1945/46 so ruins would, perhaps, be more accurate. The homestead was beyond repair. Such a tragedy as this two-storied stone building had obviously been a masterpiece of construction. Years of endearment, toil and sweat would have had been spent on these buildings by masons and stone cutters of repute. A patchwork of round and flat, grey and brown stones, some glistening as the sunlight caught their quartz content, made up each wall of the homestead and haggard. One should never attempt to break them into pieces I had been told. They are made of granite gneiss some of the oldest rock formation in Europe.

A PINCH OF SALTEE

When occupied by the tenants no more than two or at most three people would have slept downstairs in the homestead. An outside stairs ascending the western gable end was still very much in evidence. Up in the loft, fodder would have been stored for winter feed. Hay and straw providing wondrous warmth for the rooms below. This loft area could well have turned into a dormitory for the extra 'help' brought in annually at harvest time. I had learnt from a most lovely and aged gentlemen, Tommy Roche, who was the last surviving person to have worked on the island, that up to thirteen people assisted during harvest. Almost all of the island was under crops those far off days.

It was still quite easy to define the rooms as both gable ends and middle transom dividing wall were still upright. The eastern end, however, had an enormous crack dissecting it. And that whole area was leaning eastwards. I thought that the house could have been struck by a bolt of lightening sometime. A rear wall with gaping windows still remained. This would have had a lean-to roof from the centre transom. Very unfortunately nothing could be done to this ruin. My powers of restoration did not extend to that level of reconstruction or finance. That was my immediate assessment.

The haggard was an exact fifteen metre square internal measurement. It wasn't easy striding this as stones, nettles and briars matched the intensity of bracken growth. Looking at the buildings from the open end of an upturned letter 'U' (in square shape) it was quite easy to reincarnate what was what.

Our big problem was what to tackle first. We had to restore something so that we could live out here. It would be impossible to undertake the jobs that we wanted to complete with continuous daily trips in and out from the mainland. Also that would become a costly affair. We were paying £25 a trip plus B & B, etc. per day!

The Little Saltee's buildings had been constructed in granite gneiss stones of varying hues with sand and lime as the bonding agent. Those stonemasons of yesteryear wove a very special magic of their own. Their prowess was only beginning to be recognised in the twentieth and twenty-first centuries, probably four centuries late. Few modern day entrepreneurs show respect for this long lost expertise. I wished to preserve all the stonework that was still upstanding and reusable. Roofs, however, would not be resplendent in Bangor Blue tiles. That would be too much of a mechanical nightmare. I would have to use other ideas and compositions.

In my perspective the buildings at the end of the haggard, once roofed, would look like two old Irish cottages. This image brought memories of Kenya flooding back into my mindset. Another cottage another place.

This was an Irish style cottage in Fort Hall, Central Province, Kenya Colony in 1953.

Having volunteered to join the forces in battling the Mau Mau terrorists, I found myself drafted into the Colonial Service as a District Officer Kikuyu Guard (DOKG) stationed at Fort Hall in the very heart of the troubles. Each D.O. was allotted a Location (Native Reserve) and mine was No11 just outside the town. We were given a grant of Str.£250 to build a house. My closest friend, John Reed (he of Johannesburg in an upcoming chapter) was one of my senior officers in the permanent administration. He too had £250 to spend. We joined up. I drew up the plans, he got the site arranged.

To be almost totally African in our approach and finalisation of our Irish style cottage we built by the 'pole and dagga' or mud and wattle method. No bricks were used. The recipe was easy to follow. We cut lengths of wattle tree (Acacia), stuck them in the ground, bound them all together with bark strips from the same trees, mixed earth and water, made mud then filled it into the lateral cavities in the walls. Allow to dry.

Three bedrooms, bathroom, loo, sitting cum dining room, fireplace, kitchen and pantry. Floors were cattle dung and mud hardened then polished. We had a half door onto a front porch. The roof was corrugated iron. Thatch would have been too dangerous. There was a war in progress and anything that could spark an incendiary crisis was best to be avoided. We gave the outside walls, once thoroughly baked in daily African sunshine, a brushing of cement. Walls were painted white, woodwork and roof green. Believe it or not, we still had money to buy furniture in the auction rooms of Nairobi on our days off.

It was a grand home and the envy of many. The most remarkable point, however, was when I revisited Fort Hall in 1988 the cottage was still standing. It was then the residence of a Kikuyu family of six. They loved it.

Ideas aplenty flooded my thoughts. The island cottages would not be painted white – their stonework was far too impressive to be covered – but new concrete barges running up the gable ends could be white. The roof, a deep green with a white cement fascia running laterally along the sides. A wooden pergola covering the cobbled walkway running along both cottages and down the west side of the haggard would look good. Up and across it some climbing roses of pinks and reds, creepers of yellow and blue, and ivy, of the variegated type, could perhaps be trained up some of the walls.

I visualised a loft occupying half the inside area. There would have been one full length originally. This would house the master bedroom with a spiral staircase and matching metal railings enclosing the loft. Beneath, a quarry tiled dining room cum office. The other half of the ground floor would be the sitting room, perhaps with weather beaten planks as flooring, snatched from the tides and deposited on our shoreline. The full height of the building should allow for plants such as hibiscus, bougainvillea and jasmine to reach for the sky. Perspex panels set in the roof would supply all the light needed for this ancient windowless building. A stable door (half door) looking out onto the haggard which, when cleaned up and planted with trees and shrubs, would provide a serene garden hide-away for domestic birds, butterflies, dragon and damsel flies and the like. Perhaps we could have a beehive and I could savour my best of all delights – comb honey?

A PINCH OF SALTEE

The picture became evermore vivid on each of our stays. Probably the constant cleaning up, clearing away of rubble and rubbish on each visit brought the final picture more prominently into perspective. I kept on telling myself it is not impossible. We will achieve it. One must dream. I have always loved a challenge and this would be my latest and probably my last.

Right through the morning I had been taking measurements, testing sturdiness, discovering ancient pieces of iron machinery and generally attempting to visualise what it had been like in the 1940's. Shirley had been assisting in trampling and beating down the lush undergrowth, which combined a mixture of brambles, nettles, weeds of all hues; taking one end of the measuring tape, defining where the gulls nests were positioned on the ground all around the haggard area, and sketching the various buildings. I was to discover, in time, that she had a fine artistic talent lurking inside of her.

Were we to be blessed with fine calm days on this island? So far we had experienced a hundred percent affirmative. Long may it last I thought to myself.

Only a single elderberry tree grew in this area. It was inside the old homestead ruin. It grew the full height of the western gable (6 m.) and nestled in the 'V' of the two internal walls. Such a shrewd seeding by an errant pigeon or blackbird I wagered.

The three pairs of Lesser Black Backs had hardly ever left their gable perches during our morning's intrusion of their personal territory. They watched us intently and called at times, to friends to come join them and have a good look!

"They are almost as dirty as geese", I remarked to Shirley as we tucked into chicken salad, cheese, biscuits and cool cans of beer. Manual work needed sustenance. I always find that my appetite is gargantuan when working at the seaside.

We ate in silence but for the regular sound of surf breaking on shore. The call of the curlew was very prominent.

A PINCH OF SALTEE

"There is so much to learn about the bird life of this island. We will have to re-read the Saltees book and any other specialising in seabirds of Ireland. Did you notice any domestic birds in your wanderings this morning?" I asked after emitting a beery burp.

"Only a few blackbirds but I found half a dozen gulls' nests at the rear of the buildings. By the way, what do you think those raised mounds were for? Their stonework is so well done".

"Oh yes, Eugene told me they were for drying the crops before sifting and cleaning. You noticed the overhang? That's to prevent vermin climbing up the walls."

After completion of our picnic and having listened to the weather report Shirley asked,

"What about exploring the shoreline down towards St. Patrick's Bridge?"

"Great idea", I agreed.

"It'll be interesting to see what flotsam and jetsam we find".

Some two hours later we had found abandoned lobster pots, fishing nets, rope, floats and an abundance of centuries old timber and various parts of wrecks.

Cormorants, with wings outstretched entrapping every wisp of breeze, curved beaked curlews and shrill voiced oyster catchers occupied the slimy green rocks at the entrance to the 'bridge'. This catchment corner of the island would undoubtedly yield a treasure trove of artefacts in the years to come. A very different odour, perhaps more strenuously tainted with salinity by the constant breezes that curled round the two sides of the island, wafted about this museum of objets d'ocean.

Close to this most northerly point of the island we discovered the old roadway up the cliffs on to a lush pasture. This must have been the outlet/inlet of all goods when the island was inhabited. I would have to ask Declan or some of the older members of the community about this I noted, in that every increasing notebook of my mind.

A PINCH OF SALTEE

Declan picked us up at the given time and questioned me on what I had got up to? What was I going to do first and when would I be needing the metal barge? I fudged my answers making us out to be even more of an enigma.

The Americans were cackling thirteen to the dozen on a menu of gannets, puffins, guillemots and 'those quaint cuddly grey seals'.

"Oh my, but did you get yourselves organised too and do all the things you wanted to? We think you're modern day Robinson Crusoes. We wish you all the luck but heck, take care."

The fifteen minute boat ride back to Kilmore Quay went mightily fast listening to that lot. Oh well – another day, another stride forward.

Shirley and little Oscar (4 months)

A PINCH OF SALTEE

Chapter Three
Hornies Landed – Building Material – Amy Jane –
First Roof – Heart Attack – Lady Sophia

"Sheep are cheap, especially mountainy ones," that's what JB told me over the phone "and I've ordered one hundred ewes and four rams for you." They would be arriving in Kilmore Quay within the week. All I had to do was make contact with a man in Kerry and they would be delivered. I could settle up on their arrival.

Now I knew for certain that the project had commenced in earnest. 'All I had to do', I liked the way JB had put it. All he had done was buy the consignment over the phone. I was left with all the hard work.

Now the friendships both Shirley and I had supposedly cemented in Kilmore would be summarily put to the test. Greg Stafford agreed to overnight the flock, or as I quickly pointed out – keep them until the tide and weather was suitable. He still agreed. Declan said he would rather bring them out in two trips aboard Tapaidh than in one in the metal barge.

"We'll drop them close off shore. They are great swimmers you know. You can guide them in from the punt. It'll be easy enough now", he added.

I agreed to let both of them know the due arrival date. Shirley was great on the tides and weather. Her knowledge of the sea was vast as she had done a lot of sailing, both cruising and competitive, in her thirties and forties. The only time I had 'been in boats' was in the Sea Scouts at Ampleforth. I also did a season's dinghy sailing in Dun Laoghaire in 1948. Not much on a c.v. I thought to myself when I knew we had to think sea and boats for our project's survival, from now on.

Most farmers live on or near their lands. Business people are usually not too far from their offices. We, however, would have a two hour drive to Kilmore Quay, make ready our boats (when we got them), pilot them, with all food, implements and whatever out to our mooring. Then transfer to a punt or dinghy of some sort to the island. Finally carry up all items, including the dinghy, over the rocky shoreline to the homestead area. Quite a daunting task! I had already heard some say 'idiotic' or 'quite mad they must be!' But in my book 'faint hearted got no one nowhere', so Confucius say!

We met Liam the transporter with our flock of sheep at Mill Road Farm. After unloading them into an adjoining field we noticed that some of the ewes were distressed, probably due to overcrowding on the journey. The majority, however, put down their heads and tucked into some fine Wexford grass. It was late afternoon and Liam wished to get on with his journey home.

I hadn't met Liam before. He was the transporter for the farmer from whom the flock had been purchased.

"I'm not too happy with quite a few of those ewes" I said to him at the rear of his trailer. "I see a number are a bit distressed like."

"Well I'll not settle the full amount as agreed then."

"That's up to you, I'm only the carrier. I'll give Jimmy whatever you say. Sure you can talk to him on his mobile anyway."

"I'll retain a certain amount until I see how the flock works out", and he agreed with my request.

I gave him my cheque for Jimmy and a generous tip for his troubles. He thanked me and said not to forget him in any other transactions. He gave me his mobile number.

Next morning JB came down from Abbeyleix to view the flock. He leaned on the fence and looked at them for a good five minutes. He then walked amongst them and I watched his mouth silently counting.

"There are at least twenty very poor ewes here that you mustn't pay for. They are not worth a pound a piece. I'll castrate the bastard!"

"Actually I left him a couple of hundred short and said I would settle the rest once they were fit, well and landed on the island", I replied.

"Shrewd bugger", he winked, "well done".

That day and the next proved no good for the sea trip. We got the first fifty off by noon on the third day. Greg had kindly and expertly shown me how to hobble them with a small loop of rope encompassing all four legs and then tied tightly up around the head. Once seen it was quite easy to do. I had the job of preparing the hanks of rope whilst Greg and Rory hobbled them. We then piled them into Greg's sheep trailer and took them down to Tapaidh, already waiting on the slipway.

It was fairly calm with only a little surge as we moored fifty metres off our western shore. Shirley and I took to the punt while Greg and Declan untied and dumped them overboard. We headed them towards the shore. They swam swiftly to the nearest rock, slithered up the first ten metres or so shaking out the frightening odour and taste of sea water. Some of course were obstinate, as sheep can be. They turned around and tried to return to Tapaidh. Shirley and I stayed in the punt rowing backwards and forwards until all arrived safely on the shore. Once there they had the entire island for their home. Grass ad lib and plenty of water.

As we returned to the harbour a westerly wind was picking up. This didn't bode well for the next trip.

"If this gets any worse you know we won't be able to land the next lot in the same place," Declan remarked to me.

"It will take a couple of hours before we have the rest ready for you. I'll phone from Greg's to see what you think, ok? Enjoy your lunch" and I winked him away.

At three o'clock that afternoon the wind wasn't any lighter. I phoned Declan who suggested he would land them on the east side, in the lee of the wind.

A PINCH OF SALTEE

"I'm up for it but they may have a longer swim you know. Make up your mind".

Greg agreed to help again. Rory would see to the milking on his own.

This time it wasn't as easy as the first. Quite a swell was running on the east side. Declan obviously knew the waters like the length of his fishing line so we remained silent in anticipation of the exact whereabouts we were to offload our cargo. There was no way Shirley and I would be safe in the punt, so we assisted in untying . All four of us grabbed a sheep each. One hand got a good hold of the wool behind the neck and the other grabbed the wool above the tail. With one mighty pull each of us lifted them over the side and dropped them as gently as possible in the sea, pointing towards the shore.

Sheep swam here, there, and everywhere. They were being hindered in their progress by a heavy surge. Some kept returning to the boat but we leant over, turned them and sent them on their way again.

Once the first three had landed on a rocky outcrop, the others seemed to get the signal and slowly but surely followed them onto dry land.

The only problem about landing at this section of the eastern shoreline was no direct way up the cliffs. There was a spur, a sort of large jutting out from the top of the cliff, which when located they would be able to file along to the grass above.

Our theory and hope was that this lot would want to get away from the cold sea as soon as possible and would therefore head for that single spur and virgin green pasture. It took twenty minutes for the first group to successfully explore the area and achieve success. Would the others follow? We waited for a good twenty minutes until all swimmers had landed. A few had returned to the boat a couple of times so we dragged them aboard. They had made their point. We lost three. They 'bottomed up' and floated away. Most probably the shock was too much for them. The morning landings had been much easier and without loss.

A PINCH OF SALTEE

Perhaps if we had waited another day then all could have been easier. It was a Dunkirkish situation. I pondered the result.

"Some you win, some you lose", said Greg as we headed away from the island.

This was quite a historic day in the island's saga. Another flock of sheep was resident. The first piece of my jigsaw 'Island of Dreams' fell into place.

The weather was stormy for the next ten days after landing the sheep so we remained in Dublin buying up tools and timber, ordering bales of sheep netting, fence poles, staples and the like. All products needed for getting the project on a roll.

Whilst ordering the sheep fencing I thought it would be prudent to order the roofing for the first two rooms that I had already measured up. We had decided to put clear sheets on the little end room, cement the floor and fit a door and window. It would, in essence, be like a conservatory. These poor walls and floors had no covering and had been completely open to the elements for fifty years. Now they would have a chance to dry out.

I had met a builder in Kilmore Quay who had recently settled there from Dublin with his family. He said he would love the job and would have the time for it within the next month. Suited us fine. He gave me the timber requirements which I then ordered from Wexford. He said he would help in bringing it out.

This time we hired Declan's metal barge. We loaded it with all the wire and fencing posts. These numbered two hundred and fifty. They were 6ft x 3" and tanalised for longevity. That meant they were pressure treated against Borer worm and breakdown from the elements. With timber, cement and corrugated sheeting the load was close on two tonnes.

The three of us loaded it onto the barge and offloaded it onto the rocks. We then laboriously carried all of it up two hundred and fifty yards to the homestead – upwards all the way.

A PINCH OF SALTEE

It was another lovely day, calm, warm without a cloud in the sky. It had to be otherwise we wouldn't be able to land this cargo. Sweat poured from us, arms ached, legs ached. Next morning, with me at any rate – everything ached. Now we knew the enormity of what lay ahead of us if the project was to survive. Would we? That, perhaps, was the question we should have been asking ourselves.

Whatever lay ahead it was satisfying to know that here, in the autumn of our first real year of endeavour, we had the ingredients to provide fencing for the live stock and building material to launch an onslaught on the restoration of the buildings.

Living next to us in Foxrock was a charming Chinese couple, Lisa and George Ho. They had a passion for fishing. At least on three days a week, during the summer, they would take their little orange inflatable down to the Coal Harbour in Dun Laoghaire and fish the waters off Dalkey Island and Killiney Bay.

One day we noticed a very smart all white new Avon inflatable on a trailer in their driveway. I couldn't help my impertinence but immediately walked over and inspected it thoroughly.

George noticed me through the window and came out to show off his new toy. His English at best is stunted.

"How you like? Nice eh?"

"Extremely smart George, and a hard bottom this time. Nice", I said.

"Slighly bigga, stronga, you like?"

"Yes, indeed. Where is old one?" questioning him. I could hear myself almost imitating him. I always do this when in the company of foreigners. It's a terrible habit. Very rude but so easy to fall into the trap.

"In back"

At this, and on the spur of the moment, I blurted out "you sell me, yes?"

"You want?"

"Yes, yes please."

"I ask Lisa."

"Good let me know soon. Good luck with your new boat. Tight lines!"

"Oh, yes, tanks."

We parted. I rushed back to tell Shirley about my little chat. She was thrilled with the prospect of getting an inflatable. We would have the perfect punt to get us onto the island from whatever boat we took or used to get us out to our mooring. And it was light enough for us to carry up the rocks. A most important factor.

It was two days later when we got a call at the front door from Lisa. I opened it,

"Come, see boat Henry".

I followed her through the house into their back garden. The little inflatable named 'Amy Jane' was lying beside their greenhouse. It had two paddles and a pump. It looked in fair condition. There were a number of repair patches quite prominent on its sides. I lifted it up. I could handle it. That meant that Shirley and I could easily carry it.

"Ideal Lisa. Perfect. You sell, yes?"

"You want? How much you pay?"

"I have no idea honestly. It's quite old, isn't it?"

"Yes, yes. Had it five years. Second hand then. How much?"

As quick as a flash I said the first figure that came into my head,

"£50, Lisa."

With that bland poker like face the Chinese have, her reply came:

"Take it. Yours now. Good luck."

I went for my wallet and took out £50 and paid her immediately. I rushed back and told Shirley. She accompanied me straight away and we carried it through Rozel and placed Amy Jane on our little patch of lawn in the back. I immediately got the camera and took a couple of shots. Our first boat. It was also the first part of the equation. We went out next day and bought a four horsepower outboard engine.

We took the boat and engine down to Kilmore Quay the following week when we had noted a high pressure system was building up on Ireland's south coast. Bob, the builder, was also available. We pumped up Amy Jane. Shirley decided to try out both boat and engine around the harbour. She handled them with aplomb.

We were to go out with Declan but he sent a message he was delayed. Laughingly I suggested to Shirley:

"Why don't you go out on your own or better, I am sure Bob will accompany you"?

They both agreed. Shirley more enthusiastically. Bob rather grudgingly.

"But what the hell," he added with a smile.

It was flat calm so I wasn't too worried about my frivolous comment at that stage.

I had a pair of binoculars with me as I had come to love watching the various seabirds in their nesting habits and therefore always carried them. I walked to the furthest and most southern point of the harbour to follow their voyage. I was becoming more and more worried as that tiny inflatable, only nine feet in length, with my beloved Shirley and our new found builder slowly vanishing into the abyss. I lost sight of the little speck in the distance. I was now more than really worried. Nearly three miles is a long way on water. What if the engine conked out? They had paddles, yes, but what if an off shore breeze suddenly got up. Where would they be blown to? All sorts of terrible thoughts swirled around my throbbing head as I jogged back to the slipway. Thankfully Declan had arrived. He was taking the twitchers money and counting them aboard. He looked up:

"Where's Shirley? I am pulling off in a moment you know" as he palmed another tenner.

A PINCH OF SALTEE

"She left in our new little inflatable to try it out. She has Bob with her. I am a little worried as I lost them in the binoculars."

"In a rubber duck?" he said with almost anger in his voice. "That's a ruddy stupid thing to do."

Ashamedly I replied: "I know".

I took a prominent position on Tapaidh with binoculars glued on the ocean ahead.

When we got approximately two-thirds of the way out I espied a little orange dot on the rocky shoreline near our landing spot. I was mightily relieved. As we neared our mooring, which Declan had kindly positioned for us on our last visit, I saw Bob push Amy Jane out into deeper water so that Shirley could start the outboard without interference with any kelp.

When she pulled up beside Tapaidh, and before I could get a word in, Declan let her have it in no uncertain manner. Stern stuff these Wexford fishermen can throw out when necessary!

Shirley, who in my opinion is exceedingly conservative and rather 'church' in her manner was somewhat taken aback. She looked at me for confidence. Wide eyes pleading.

"It's ok my darling. A stupid thing to have done. I shouldn't have let you but what a historic and happy ending. Well done" as I handed down our picnic box and a few odds and ends. A number of the passengers showed their appreciation of her heroics. The tension subsided.

"That was a bit rich from Declan when he was the reason I came on ahead." Shirley sounded furious as she shouted to me over the noise of the outboard.

This was my first time in Amy Jane and despite getting a thoroughly wet bottom I appreciated her usefulness and adaptability. We had no trouble in carrying her up the rocks. I carried the outboard on its own.

That day Bob fashioned the timbers for our first roof. I handed him up the lengths of clear plastic corrugated sheeting which made our general purpose room a virtual conservatory. May the sun shine eternally on the Saltees I said to myself.

We slept at Mill Road that night after excellent fresh fish platters which then lead on to quite a session at Kehoes. I, however, did not sleep well. What a fool I had been in allowing Shirley and Bob to boat out to the island in Amy Jane. We hadn't even tried her on a long trip. She could have sprung a leak out in the bay and miles from anyone. What then? Even though both of them were wearing life jackets.

During the remaining weeks of autumn we managed to make quite a few trips out to the island. I have always thought that September – October are two of our nicest months. Luckily this year proved me correct.

Bob had enough time to complete the two roofs, the doors, the window shutter and had cemented the floor of the end room. I had designed a folding double bed which we constructed in situ. It fitted along the wall opposite the fireplace and beneath the little window. When not in use the bed could be a single bunk or a table. We had found a folding table/shelf up in the attic at Rozel which we placed in another corner of the room. There wasn't much space for anything really but we, at least, could now sleep out there.

In the adjoining room we cleared out all the muck from the floor. Lo and behold we found a real cobbled stone floor – the cow shed no doubt! Along one wall we built a wide shelf. This would be our kitchen and store room.

We bought a two ring gas cooker, a small camping refrigerator, also gas, and a double lilo. Over the next couple of trips we managed to bring out all the necessities to maintain body and soul. We were now resident. The project was on 'go'.

It was probably best to put the island into the background during those long upcoming winter months. Luckily both rooms had been completed, doors locked with all our first summer's purchases stored within. An ancient iron bath had been placed outside to collect rain water. Roll on next spring was our only thought.

I went to writing class, Shirley to watercolour class. I put a lot down on paper regarding the island project which we then discussed with JB on trips to Abbeyleix.

During one of these winter visits to Blandsfort JB brought up the idea of us taking a holiday in the sun. He and I would discuss this subject at length each winter. His trips, visiting me in far off Africa and India had whetted his appetite for adventure.

"You two look as if you need to get away", he said with sincerity.

We had indeed been thinking along these lines as I had an invitation to judge and commentate the South African Eventing Championships (equestrian) in Johannesburg that April. I had been out to do the same job, a most pleasant task, the year before but on my own. I wanted to see my daughter, son-in-law and grandchildren who were living in Underberg, Natal as well as showing the country I loved so much to Shirley.

After calling up a few of my old friends in South Africa they arranged a really exciting sounding trip encompassing the Eastern Transvaal game reserves, an equestrian safari and then finally a trip to Sun City for golf and gambling. We were both looking forward to almost three weeks of sun.

I flew out two days ahead as I had a heavy round of PR duties to perform for the sponsors, SAPPI. (South African Pulp and Paper Industries) who were paying my expenses. These duties included an early morning t.v. appearance, two radio interviews, meeting the local press and a ride around the event course at Inanda Country Base, Kyalami. The latter I had managed to put off 'till Shirley arrived as I knew she would love to see the types of jumps and terrain used under African skies and twenty-eight degrees.

A PINCH OF SALTEE

It had been a pretty hectic twenty-four hours prior to my collecting Shirley at Johannesburg International Airport and then being driven to our holiday cottage in the northern suburb of Hyde Park. We rested for the remainder of the morning and then walked, about a mile, up to the shopping centre which I had opened with plenty of pomp and ceremony some fifteen years previously.

I'd had a very successful television career in Johannesburg and had become what some people call a 'celebrity'! I enjoyed television immensely and whatever extras came from that exposure I was mightily grateful for. It all helped to pay for my equestrian exploits.

We had an enjoyable Italian lunch, window shopped and bought ourselves some new paperbacks for the holiday ahead. Shirley found the climate a bit hot so took to the coolth of our bedroom. I changed into bathing shorts, rolled out a lounger and took up residence at the swimming pool in our cottage's back garden.

That evening we had been invited to a party by the resident Irish Times correspondent, Patrick Laurence, and his wife who had already interviewed me for a local paper. It was a quiet three-couple dinner party, an excellent curry with superb desserts to follow, a most relaxing evening. We were dropped back at our cottage at midnight.

Our plans for the morning were an early breakfast and then to be collected at 8.30am, taken to the event course and headquarters where we would be given two horses and a guide. I like to ride the course as it gives me, as commentator, a feel for what both horse and rider will encounter as they compete over an exacting three and a half miles at competition speed.

I awoke around 7.00am as usual, got up put the kettle on and went for a stroll in the garden to test the temperature of the pool. Perhaps, I thought, a dip before breakfast would be on the cards.

A PINCH OF SALTEE

Roiboss is the local South African herbal tea. Its name stared out from the shelf at me so I brewed up two mugs. Shirley might like it. I adored it. One of the books I had purchased yesterday – Kookie Gelmann's latest – had really got my attention and I was looking forward to a quick extra read for a half an hour or so before breakfast. Shirley was still asleep. After about five minutes I felt a tightening across my chest and a definite unease in my breathing. I got up and went to look in my wash bag for an antacid. It must be a severe bout of indigestion I thought. Suddenly nausea took hold of me. I was now perspiring and making a lot of noise. Shirley awoke and enquired as to what was the matter:

"I think it is indigestion. I am having trouble breathing and I'm sweating like a stuck pig", I replied between oops, huffs and puffs.

"How is your left arm. Do you feel it paining by any chance"?

"Yes, it's tingling, like pins and needles" was my halting reply.

She got out of bed and comforted me as best she could between my gulps, gasps and attempts at getting some air into a painful set of lungs. The towel I clutched in my right hand was already sodden from the gallons of sweat I had lost.

Shirley was dressing. She said she would go to the big house and phone a doctor. I prayed that I didn't need one.

Just as sudden as the nausea had started, so it abated. I stood up and with gasps and gulps becoming less frequent, managed a few sips of tea. Whilst Shirley was in the big house I dressed, washed and shaved myself, telling myself I was going riding in less than an hour.

"Can you believe this", she said with frustration written all over her pretty face. "But they haven't used a doctor in twenty years and don't know how to get hold of one!"

"Thank God you didn't find the yellow pages," I joked with her.

A PINCH OF SALTEE

I was still hesitant in my breathing and the tightness across the chest was strange.   My breathing became worse.   I started to perspire again. It was after 8.00am and we were being collected in twenty minutes time by an old friend of mine, Sharon Trail. Shirley was adamant that I see a doctor so I compromised. Sharon, I knew, would have a G.P. and could take us to him.

That's exactly what transpired but here was where the comedy of errors really started.

Sharon's own GP was away in Capetown but his partner, a lady doctor, was on duty. It took ten minutes before she had all the details. She went for the ECG machine, put all the pads on me – it didn't work. She tried a second time. No luck. She asked the sister to please find the other machine. It was brought after an another five minutes delay. It was switched on. Not a blink or bleep. "Try again" the sister said. Still no go. Even I was getting a little worried at this point as I began to realise that it was not indigestion but something to do with my heart.

The sister was asked to take me to Mill Park Hospital as Sharon had already left to meet a previous appointment. She agreed. I heard the charming but now terribly embarrassed and frustrated doctor tell Shirley that she would phone ahead and have a cardiologist awaiting me.

My breathing was still difficult and the tightness was becoming more severe as I walked into the hospital's reception area. They were ready for me. Swing doors opened to my left. Two large strong looking nurses guided a trolley towards me, picked me up, and fast forwarded me back through those doors into ICU. Shirley was left to do the necessary paperwork at reception.

I was immediately given an ECG which worked properly, met the cardiologist, and allocated a bed.

Shirley came to see me sometime later. Now stable, I felt such a fool at causing all this concern. She was very, very worried as she was all alone in a strange country. It showed in her face I was well covered by insurance and Shirley had signed various

48

papers for the hospital administration detailing all this. But she was distraught and didn't know who to turn to.

I suggested the Reeds, John and Iona who I had introduced her to on our way from the airport.

They had a lovely house in the Chelsea style suburb of Melville which, as Shirley found out later, was within walking distance of the hospital

It must have been the most trying time for Shirley. Her world and holiday turned upside down. She was literally on her own. And she was five thousand miles from Dublin. I felt miserable for her.

On my fourth day in hospital I had my angiogram. This was quite amusing. I had 'clicked' from the off with my Cardio, and he explained to me what I was about to see on the screen

"See those Henry", pointing to a line of bumps and humps,

"Yes. They look like a string of Denny sausages", I jokingly replied.

"A good analogy and I know what you are talking about. I have lectured twice in Dublin. I love your full Irish breakfast by the way".

"Well, I never", was all I could think of answering.

"How many sausages can you count?"

"One – two – three- four. Four sausages Your Reverence", I replied with a smirk and a peal of laughter.

"Quite correct. That means a quadruple bypass young man." And with that he moved majestically out of the theatre.

The nurses wheeling me back to my ward said the op would be performed either tomorrow or next day. Not to worry. It's really very easy these days.

That afternoon, just after Shirley had departed from her daily visit, I was introduced to the surgeon. A fine athletically fit man of about forty-five with smiling eyes. He was Afrikaans. After explaining the procedure to me he got up off the bed and said:

A PINCH OF SALTEE

"Most probably tomorrow morning and we'll have you out in ten days. O.K. Meneer? Goud"!

Later that evening the ward sister came to my bed and explained that the operation wouldn't be, as hoped, in the morning.

"It's just a twenty-four hour postponement," as she wished me a pleasant night's sleep.

Our little ward had French doors out onto a pristine lawn with rose beds all around. Shirley and I spent all her visiting time out there. I wasn't in the slightest bit anxious about the operation. All I wished was, for it to be over. Perhaps we could enjoy a little holiday as well as my recuperation before returning to Ireland. The island, and my future plans for it, was very much on the forecourt of my mind. Would I be able to complete or even carry out the workload I had envisaged? I, however, was more worried about my beloved Shirley who was visibly losing weight and getting rivers of worry lines below her usually sparkling eyes. She was my rock and continued to bolster my confidence. It was her who needed constant boosting right now – that especial TLC in these trying times. She was left to battle the external alien elements of a country and life she didn't understand. I, on the other hand, was being cosseted by a high tech system and caring staff. Who was getting the best deal I questioned myself?

Twenty-four hours later I was duly prepared for the operation and after various injections was wheeled into theatre. My only memory was of partial awakening sometime somewhere and fighting with whatever was in my mouth.

Finally I slowly opened my eyes. At the foot of my bed was a smiling Shirley. I hope I reciprocated the smile.

I was in the land of living. That's all I saw. I was away again into never, never land. It was very dark when I next awoke. No part of me hurt. No pain.

Next time I awoke it was breakfast for those who were a day or two post operative. I was thirsty. Hot sweet tea was all I needed. And I got it.

A PINCH OF SALTEE

The horse trials had long passed. I had let the sponsors down. I needed to know the results. That's all that was galloping around my cotton wool lined mind. No pain anywhere. I couldn't believe my luck

I returned from a wonderful snooze to find my son Patrick, daughter Deirdre and son-in-law Robert with Shirley all standing at the bottom of my bed. The family had driven up from Natal during the night and would be staying for two days. They looked very tired.

I had entered hospital five days previously, fairly fit, not over weight, with normal blood pressure and an average cholesterol level. I wasn't a smoker and didn't drink to any great extent. Stress, whatever that meant or covered, must have been the enemy. My attitude then was: I've had the op! let's get on with getting better. Listen to the doctors and carry out their recommendations. I wanted to be fit and well again, out of here and into the sunshine. I have always been an optimist so here goes, I said to myself, let me prove it.

I was up and walking around after three days. My physiotherapist put me through her paces. She was petite with auburn hair, freckled cream-like skin, sparkling bright blue eyes. She had to be Irish. She was stern but sweet. She told me to walk once around the hospital block, outdoors in the morning and again in the afternoon. But of course my exercises, which she had already shown me, were to be taken seriously and as many times a day as possible. All this jazzed me up. I got a real buzz out of getting well.

My appetite was equine in proportion, consuming everything that was served up and more. My most welcome visitors brought lots of goodies I hadn't tasted for ages – Kooksisters, melk tert and biltong[10] from my Afrikaans friends,

---

[10] Sticky sweets used as a dessert, milk tart with cinnamon and dried venison meat cut into small strips.

supplemented by bowls of fruit, homemade biscuits and sinful fudge! That I kept for Shirley.

She visited for hours each day and set about reorganising the rest of our 'holiday'. She too had come through the trauma with amazing strength. She found what sounded like a lovely country house accommodation, Apricot Hills, with swimming pool and acres of gardens, in the mountains some thirty miles north-west of Johannesburg. We would move there on my being released. That happened ten days after the operation. It was bliss. Shirley managed to get a day's riding in a nearby game reserve.

Unfortunately, however, all good things do come to an end. We had so enjoyed our sojourn at Apricot Hills but then came a ghastly phone call and the urgent request from my medical insurance company. They required me to return to Ireland as soon as possible, although the local medics thought I should recuperate for a longer time. This obviously upset me as I became ill on the way to the airport ending up in a wheelchair. We got upgraded onto a different airline and given, what turned out to be, a horrific and ridiculous flight path home. Without doubt, this became the most stressful period of the entire operation.

On returning to Dublin, Shirley put me straight to bed. She herself was totally exhausted and distraught. But we were home. All she did to cheer both of us up was to collect Oscar from his 'hotel' in Kilmacanogue. After inspecting the house and all his toys he joined me on the bed. He couldn't believe his luck.

She took my temperature a couple of hours later and found it high. She called my doctor whose locum arrived within the hour. I was fast asleep.

I awoke to find someone feeling my pulse. On opening my eyes I thought I was back in that Johannesburg hospital – I must still be dreaming. My mind was a troubled ocean of turbulent currents. Here was a lady doctor holding my hand and she was black. Had she accompanied me on the trip? Had I really left

A PINCH OF SALTEE

South Africa? What was going on? All these and more flashed across my bedraggled mind screen – reception was not digital.

"Yes, his temperature is high. I'm ringing the hospital and he should go in straight away. Can you take him?" I heard the doctor asking Shirley.

When that was settled I dared to ask the doctor where she came from.

"Zimbabwe", she replied, "but I have been in Dublin for nine years. Why you ask?"

"Oh, I am an ex Rhodesian too. What part are you from?"

"Umtare. You knew it as Umtali".

"Indeed I did, my daughter was born there."

I then broke into Cindebele, a common colloquial language spoken by the majority of Africans in my day. She replied. We spoke ethnically for another few minutes and then she bade us farewell. What an amazing experience! I asked myself the question 'is fact not a lot more strange than fiction?' I agreed 'it was'.

Shirley took me to St.Vincent's Hospital where I had been checked in by the locum. I was running a high temperature so blood samples were taken.

I spent nine days in hospital feeling better but more frustrated each day. Blood samples were taken three times a day. No one could find anything whatsoever wrong – medically – with me. I just ran a high temperature each evening. I finally gave them an ultimatum.

"I'm getting a taxi at lunchtime unless consultants et al give reasons for my further confinement". All who had been attending me – cardiologist, G.P., matron and sisters – huffed and puffed around me all morning.

At noon I got the all clear.

"You may go home. But ask your wife to take your temperature each evening and let us know if anything untoward should occur".

53

A PINCH OF SALTEE

They didn't look pleased. I was. And after all I was vacating a bed for someone more needful.

The temperature remained normal from that day on. Shirley and I put it all down to 'post operative stress' and that must cover a myriad of sins!

We were now almost halfway through the year. I had a strict 'get fit' discipline to adhere to each day. Walk for twenty minutes a.m. and then twenty minutes p.m. Thank God I had Oscar. He took over my recuperation and lead me on my daily exercise. I achieved an hour a day by the end of May. I enjoyed every stride. I was becoming stronger each day. And these times of solitude allowed for island plans to resurface and formulate.

. All my island thoughts of the previous few weeks came flooding into vision. Fencing had to be stretched across the island; waterholes had to be dug out and enlarged; the Kerrys would be arriving in a couple of months; one of the cottages must be roofed; the homestead area had to be fenced to keep rabbits and stock out; sheep had to be shorn, lambs taken to the mainland. I was not allowed to do any manual work. Great I thought to myself "how on earth do I get it all done, and I must".

Good news arrived. JB phoned to say that my REPS plan had been accepted. Little Saltee was to receive its first income. The heart attack, however, could not have come at a more inopportune moment. Perhaps, however, things were looking up.

Two very significant items then occurred on a single day in early June. And two important decisions were made.

I got a letter from Eugene Wallace outlining what I might do to protect the various bird species that were nesting on the lands of the island, i.e. Cormorants, Shear Waters and Puffins. He thought it would be advantageous to fence off the stone walls occupied for nesting purposes and an area on the south-west of the island for the burrowers – Shear Waters and Puffins. It wasn't obligatory but probably prudent!

54

A PINCH OF SALTEE

Whilst I was in South Africa I discussed this very problem with various friends who were involved in wild life preservation, as I had been myself for the thirty years previously. They thought it would be wrong to fence in areas for nesting purposes only as there were too many negatives present.

I had already observed how the young Cormorants, who were now nesting on the walls instead of the cliffs, battled through the bracken in attempting to reach the cliffs edge before their maiden flights. Cormorants are not the greatest walkers. I would count them as wobblers at that stage of their maturity! It was my opinion, that if I put a mesh fence, say some five metres away from the nests the Cormorant chicks, who have an enormous wing span, they would get caught up in the fence and die in their tens.

I therefore decided to stretch a fence across the middle of the island from east to west. This would allow the stock to be kept in the northern portion of the island when nesting was taking place in the southern areas. This fence, however, had to be strung across a seven hundred metre stretch with a couple of concertina gates inserted in it. Pray who was to do it? It would need a team of three at least to handle the task.

The second important item was the arrival of the free newspaper 'The Southsider' through our letterbox. I had never previously indulged in its content but this time I did. Perhaps fate? Therein I read a small 'for sale' advertisement for a fifteen foot fibreglass fishing boat, two outboard engines and trailer. I phoned the number, located its whereabouts and said: "I'm on my way. Please hold it for me."

Now, as I have already stated I am not a boatman or sailor but I liked what I saw. Shirley did too.

"It will be perfect for us, not too big, easy to handle and we get two engines. Go for it. I'll leave you to barter" and with that Shirley took Oscar for a walk around the estate. It was Clondalkin.

Some thirty minutes later I came out of the house and called Shirley to meet Paul Mulhall.

A PINCH OF SALTEE

"I have concluded the deal, my darling. All we have to do now is get a tow bar. Thanks a ton Paul. We'll collect her in a day or two. Cheers", I said as I returned to the car.

We discussed our new purchase at length on the drive home. I wished to name her *'Lady Sophia'* after my grandmother who was given the island by her mother. Shirley agreed. 'Sophie', as she would be known, was the perfect partner for 'Amy Jane'.

"Do you realise we are now independent, my love. All we have to do is charm the harbour master, get a berth in the marina and we'll be set fair".

"I'll leave that up to you. I'll sort out all the marine items that we'll need", replied Shirley with a Salty seafaring smirk. I thought she was as chuffed as I was.

Jim McGillicuddy arriving!

Farm Ruins untouched for 53 Years

See last two pictures for update

Shirley's Waterhole as found in 1996.
Tommy McLoughlin and Eugene Wallace looking on.

Two years later.

Our sandy beach.

The first consignment of fence posts and wire.

The Long Haul

Our home for the first 3 years

**First sheep on trip to island aided by
Rory and Greg Stafford.**

Part of the flock on north side of fenceline.

Shirley, Tony and Patrick at first shearing.

Organic lamb en route to mainland.

Well cushioned for
Kerry heifers.

At sea – quite rough crossing

Land Ahoy !

This is the Life !

Saltee Lttle Lady – the first born.

Herd awaiting their treats.

Above and Below - The tools of our trade.

Chapter Four

Agricultural Dept. Inspections – REPS – Farm Work – Patrick – Selecting Kerries – The Voyage

June '99 started off a very busy month. It continued at such a pace that I never had a moment to think about the heart attack of two months previous. In my mind it was now a thing of the past. I just kept on attempting to get fitter and fitter. Having had my REPS plan accepted, the island farm had to now have a dividing stock proof fence, two water holes cleared and ready for cattle and sheep and work to be commenced on the restoration of our first stone wall.

I now felt the bureaucratic might of our agricultural department. The first phone call was from the Livestock Section informing me to expect a visit from one of their inspectors regarding my Headage and Ewe Premium application. With a registered flock of sheep, I was entitled to claim payment on the number of ewes on the farm. This number had to be verified. Hence an official inspection.

A couple of days later I received another call, from Donal O'Brien who would be coming to inspect the flock. And when would it be convenient? That was up to the weather and tides I told him but we agreed on a day the following week. I would confirm if all was well.

Shirley was now monitoring weather forecasts on the internet which gave us an advanced four-day overview. These were to prove invaluable in the years ahead.

Donal was brought out to our mooring by Declan at 11.15am. It was a lovely sunny calm day. Shirley took out 'Amy Jane' to collect him. I had warned Donal about how difficult it was in reaching the island. It didn't seem to deter him. Not even the jungle like density of bracken which he saw, on either side of the pathway, was what he would have to grapple with on his quest to count our flock.

Donal was a fine big framed agricultural man. He wore a cotton hat which had seen much better days. Pulled down tight to save it from flying off his head in the wind. When bare headed I could see that the hat was essential wear on hot summer days. His brown hair was thinning. On his forehead I noticed a definite tan line created by the hat band. Two-tone foreheads are the stamp of men working outdoors. Well kitted, his wellies kept him dry.

After a mug of tea he set off with Shirley to find the sheep, then to count them. I remained at the homestead and pottered about with ideas and measurements of my plans for shrubs, trees and creepers. Where best to plant them, how to protect them. Oscar stayed with me. He wasn't yet trained to herd sheep and would therefore have been more of a hindrance.

It was an hour and a half later when I saw them atop the hill that overlooks the homestead. There were chatting away as friends of many moons would. I had cool beers awaiting them. One of our most worthwhile purchases, bought through Buy n' Sell Magazine, was an old, almost antique, camping gas fridge which worked off a tiny cylinder. It was just big enough to hold one litre milk, a small butter, three beers and some sandwiches. This we left out on the island. Shirley always packed essential and immediate items in a soft cool bag which we carried ashore each time. We, and any guests, were therefore adequately provided for.

Donal and I discussed the island, our plans for farming it, and how many sheep did I think I had? I showed him my notebook from the previous autumn, the dates they arrived, the various counts we had attempted and the latest number of lambs.

"It's not easy getting an accurate count is it", he remarked as he studied my notes.

"Well I counted fifty odd in a group down on the south-east side. Another big group of forty odd on the west and a third of forty-something quite close to here", he muttered as he added up figures he had jotted down in his little note book. "Shirley saw another lot close to a waterhole but she couldn't get an accurate count. Anyhow the good news is that you have more than your application asked for". If I had more than the number applied for, I would qualify for the grant.

He then took out some official forms, filled in certain figures and asked "sign here please. Keep that in your herd register book when you get it". I asked if that was it and he said "Yea, not too arduous a task?" he questioned.

Shirley arrived at our makeshift table and chairs with sandwiches and more beer. Donal then proceeded to give us insights into many of the farms and farmers in and around Kilmore Quay. Looking out from our Mediterranean-like site onto the mainland, he could pick out landmarks which he pinpointed for us to locate when we toured the local town lands.

On leaving, he once again assisted Shirley in carrying 'Amy Jane' and the outboard. We remained on the island as the weather was warm and a lot of work had to be done.

My son Patrick and his fiancée, Liezel, had moved to England the previous year. They were working on an enormous horticultural establishment in East Anglia. Patrick had been over for a brief visit during the previous summer and said he would be available for a month or so if and when I needed him. In my book that was now. He would be the ideal man for the job – the job of erecting the stock fence.

I phoned him up. He thought it a great idea and could probably bring a friend or two to help in any work that was needed. We planned his arrival for July.

It was the following week, we were once again back in Dublin when I got the second call from the Agricultural Department. This time it was from the REPS Section out of Enniscorthy. They would be sending an inspector, when please? I gave them the same answer as before. Ten days later there was another high pressure approaching the south-east so I contacted them to organise the day and time.

Declan, this time, brought out Jim McGillicuddy and introduced him to Shirley at our mooring. Declan had a full boat of tourists bound for the big island. Oscar and I were on the shore in expectation of them. Oscar moved from rock to rock, swimming between them while anxiously watching his 'mummy' sailing away in 'Amy Jane'! Every now and then he would pull up a piece of kelp, like a small branch of a tree, and drag it towards me. His eyes pleading to throw it for him.

The return trip in 'Amy Jane' didn't look to be going smoothly as I saw a lot of activity. Jim was bailing furiously as Shirley guided the dinghy. They did seem, from afar, somewhat agitated. This was not at all like Shirley. I could see that she was instructing our visitor in what to do. To my relief they landed safely.

Jim helped to carry the dinghy and engine up the shoreline. Shirley was jabbering away as I met them. Jim didn't look too pleased with things – a lot different to Donal who had been completely laid back.

"You won't believe what happened. Somehow the little bung got kicked out and we started taking in gallons of water. Poor Jim had to bale for all he was worth as I tried to retrieve and return it whilst steering the little blighter. Not an easy journey I can tell you."

"Oh Jim, I am so sorry. Are you both ok?" was all I could muster as I thought about the horror of what might have been.

"Yes, I'm fine and Shirley was tremendous. She was so reassuring. She made me feel safe. Mind you I wouldn't want a repeat performance."

We checked the plug hole and bung and both seemed tight again. We agreed to check them again before the return trip. I thought we all needed a drink of something strong but mugs of hot tea were requested.

A PINCH OF SALTEE

Jim was somewhat quiet at the outset which I put down to the recent mishap. A tall lean freckle-faced man with wavy ginger hair tinged with grey flowed back from a well tanned forehead. He thawed within the hour as he listened to my reasons for being behind in putting my REPS plan into operation. It was just that – my medical operation – which had got in the way.

I had, during the winter, drawn out in sketch form plans for the fence, waterholes and the stone wall that had to be restored as stated in my plan.

My farm briefcase was packed full with project analysis, maps, notes, a diary and receipts. These proved that all the fencing poles, implements and nails had been purchased the previous year from the Wexford Co-op and were in situ. Shirley and I had knocked in approximately two dozen poles last autumn outlining the route the fence would take. I told Jim that Shirley would take him on a tour of the island and show him all the places we would be working on. I would follow but wouldn't be able to cover the ground they could.

"There will be food and drink ready for you on your return. Don't get lost", I jeered as they set out up the hill. Oscar was already ahead of them and rabbiting on with his daily delight, hunting.

I was making good progress with my daily walk load. On the island I had two alternatives. The now well worn route up the hill to either *Shirley's* (waterhole) and onto the southern pastures which were not overrun with high bracken was more preferable than heading southwards battling through uncharted oceans of fern. If I took Oscar on his lead he would up the pace which made me walk faster and that, in turn, made my breathing much heavier which allowed me to inhale more ozone. My fitness rose to a level I felt allowed me to tackle more arduous work loads. I was determined to be ahead of the field in the recuperation stakes. Shirley, Oscar and ultimately that of the island were my life. They formed the trigger that would fire me into a rapid reincarnation. And also that of the island.

A PINCH OF SALTEE

Jim was 'gob smacked' by the extent of our project. Shirley had obviously been thorough in her explanation and definition of our plans. He fully appreciated what we were attempting and "from what I can see you will achieve. I have nothing but admiration". We felt very proud of ourselves.

We accompanied him back to Kilmore Quay and partook in a fine meal well washed down in the crowded warmth of our village 'office'. On parting I took his arm and said "I promise to have the REPS work completed by August. Please return then and see for yourself". This was quite a challenge I thought to myself.

We returned to Dublin that evening and it was three days later when I answered the phone and listened to thirty seconds 'As gaeilge'. I went silent with no reply. I had indeed learnt Irish at St. Gerrard's and could still say my prayers in it but, at that moment, I could not think in Irish.

A quiet light voice said "I thought you were an islander?" I could feel the smile in that sentence. It was of course Jim McGuillicudy.

"You caught me out James", I replied, "but if I'd said 'dia linn' what would you have said in return".

"That I hadn't sneezed" and he roared with laughter. "And God bless you too"!

We chatted for a few minutes about the Irish language and how the island was not in the Gaeltacht.

"Well, I've good news for you. Your plan is accepted totally now. So go to it".

I replied in Irish "go raibh mile maith agat". We both chortled as we terminated our conversation.

I had been warned by JB, earlier in the year, that according to the conditions of my grant I might well be inspected. I was grateful therefore that both had met with approval. It brought to the fore the old adage 'honesty is the best policy'. Also the island would, later in the year, receive its second increment, that of the Ewe Premium, I had already applied for. Things were looking up.

A PINCH OF SALTEE

It was now almost the end of June and I was awaiting a call from Patrick. Opportunely it came. His news wasn't the greatest, however, as he told me his Aussie and New Zealand friends who had wanted to come over had both cried off but he did have another Australian who would love the change. I said fine and who was he?

"He's a she, Dad. As big as me, a farm girl and immensely strong".

I took a couple of silent gulps before replying "Pat, this is not a holiday I'm afraid. This is going to be hard work and it has to be done by a certain date as I have already told you –its very important, please understand

"Not a problem Dad. Cathy lives with us. We all share a mobile home. She's really up for it. You should see her workload each shift and then you'd know what I'm talking about."

I couldn't very well argue with him. I needed the job done and if he said they would complete it – no sweat – then I had to trust him.

"O.K.", I said "but remember work first, play later. No excuses now".

Cathy and Patrick arrived on due date in Kilmore Quay. On setting foot on the island Pat strung up the only double tent that we had. I suggested he site it in one of the roofless cottages in the haggard which would be well sheltered. We walked the line of the forthcoming fence measuring off where the posts would go and the two concertina gates positioned. Now it was up to them to carry up all the rolls of mesh wire and the two hundred or so fence poles. They didn't seem daunted by the task ahead.

Cathy was a pretty girl. She was tall, well proportioned, rather shy with a set of shoulders that I wouldn't like to be on the receiving end of. I warned my strapping 6' 2" raw boned South African son. He smiled back at me.

I was feeling remarkably fit and well so decided to join them as a team member. We had worked out that the three of us were essential as two would be needed to strain the wire whilst the third, me, hammered staples into the fence posts. Shirley was kept busy strimming the bracken for this historical fence building operation. We completed it, coast to coast, after ten full working days. We were blessed with fine warm sunny weather.

I was so thrilled to have worked with my son. We hadn't had much chance of doing that in his maturing years although he had joined me on both farms for many months in Kenya in the late eighties. Patrick is a born naturalist and spent many hours explaining the habits of our bird colonies to Cathy. They also spent time fishing and swimming in the days prior to their departure. It was a successful enterprise. I drove them to Rosslare to catch the ferry back to Fishguard. From there they would entrain all the way across England to East Anglia. Cathy said she would be flying off to Australia within six months, probably for Christmas, but that she would love to return to see more of Ireland. Her mother was alone on their small holding and would be looking forward to her return.

Once they had strapped on their 'backpacks' I asked them to close their eyes and stretch their right arms out to me with one hand on top of the others'. I then placed sterling £500 in notes into them and closed their fingers tight around it.

"Share that as best you think. Thanks a million. It was great having you both. Do come again Cathy. Maybe bring your mum next time? See you soon son. God Bless". I wrapped my arms around him.

Not a word was said. Tears were close. Surprise was evident. My gratitude hopefully showed through. I hate goodbyes.

Shirley had started on the restoration of the stone wall leading up from the haggard to the top of the hill. We found that fifty years of wind and rain had moved a lot of soil onto the wall. A good number of stones had also been blown off and rested on either side. They in turn had been covered over with grass and bracken. This was not going to be an easy job. Shirley said, however, she was up to it. What a treasure I repeated to myself.

It was a joy to be independent in the boat department. Now that we had the two main ingredients it meant we were able to, not only plan our trips to our liking but with perusal of the Tidal Timetable, boat out whenever it was best and most convenient for us. By that I mean – take the tide at its highest therefore having less distance to carry things up the shore. Declan had specific times for departure and collection of tourists. Up until then we had to adhere to his business schedule even if it meant unsuitability for us at landing on the island. He had been, however, very kind to us from the outset and indeed assisted us in every way possible. A grand rapport was bonding in our friendships.

Our next big project was to bring out all the timber and roofing for the cottage. I hired Declan's metal barge again and with the help of the builder and a couple of school leavers Shirley and I loaded and off loaded the cargo – once again!

The builder managed to put up all the rafters and beams for loft and roof before the stormy season set in. These timbers would mellow through the winter and be available for flooring and roofing the coming year. I was beginning to realise that, with all the best intentions, it was unlikely that my work schedule would be completed in my intended time chart. I had to learn to be patient, not something that had been in my book of life up 'till now, but I loved a challenge

At around the same time we had brought out the load of timber JB phoned to ask:

"What about the Kerries? Did I feel up to it yet?"

"Of course," says I "when and where?"

"Come down by train. I'll meet you at Portlaois and we'll set off for Killarney together. We'll need a couple of days away."

A PINCH OF SALTEE

It was years since I had been on a train at home so the trip to Killarney was mouth watering.   Such landscapes, such greenness. No wonder the tourists love this land of ours.

We discussed the pros and cons of the countryside.

"Remember all those neat hedgerows of Wales and England JB – well what's your opinion, their way or ours"

"Both have their plusses but well kept probably outweighs unkempt.   Farmers in UK were always more advanced in their rural rules of tidiness – they, in the main, were also richer, so could afford to maintain fences and ditches to a high standard."

"I wouldn't want to see everywhere neat and tidy but also not overgrown and out of control," I ended with.

I also noted the lack of coloured dairy breeds – everything was now black and white.   Where were the Ayrshire, Jersey, Guernsey and Shorthorn of our childhoods? Sheep were sparse, save for the hills we passed through.   Tillage seemed to stop outside Kildare.

"And what was all that unploughed land?"

"That's setaside. The EU doesn't want over production of anything so they pay the farmer to not grow crops!" I hadn't heard of that concept before. It seemed mighty strange to me.   I had been used to the maxim 'produce as much as you can' – it still wouldn't be enough for Africa and India.

"You'll be required to do something similar on the island with stocking levels. Only a certain unit ratio per hectare. By the way do you know how many acres to the hectare? I know you still think in all the old lingo".

"Two point something" I replied. I'll never be able to get all these kilos and hectares into my numb skull brain. I'm too old fashioned. Too lazy most probably. Like I never agreed with the Mass in English. A wonderful ceremony in Latin, so majestic. I let out a burst of *Credo in unum deum.*   This received some amazing stares from those in the carriage who were without earphones. I smiled back.

A PINCH OF SALTEE

JB and I spent the next hour reminiscing on Ampleforth and our time spent in North Wales. Those years seemed only yesterday, then we kept opening envelopes of memories. Those marked *par avion* brought tales of JB's visits to me in Kenya and India.

Whilst in Kenya we had sped around the country – had photographed ourselves standing astride the equator; amongst Flamingos at Lake Elementeita; hippos and cheetah at Nakuru; herds of wildebeest, zebra, giraffe, elephant and two prides of lion on the Maasai Mara; antelope, too many to categorise, and a meal of crocodile meat at the famous Carnivore Restaurant in Nairobi.

India and Goa had been less hectic as JB had brought his charming artistic wife, Anna, to visit us. We lazed on the sparsely populated coral beaches of Goa, partaking in the spiced delicacies of the region.

JB shot a home movie on the farm I managed outside Bangalore and Anna took home a portfolio of sketches. On a trip up country to Ooti we viewed herds of elephants and had the amazing good fortune of watching a male tiger cross the road in front of us at a very leisurely pace. We had sunshine every day.

A vivid canvas of volcanic proportion unfolded in our archive of friendship.

Killarney was somewhat different. Jarvies were slower than those in India; streets were a lot cleaner; fast fry odours lacked spiciness. I missed the curries and Byrianiis. My nostrils craved for those erotic nasal thrills. It was raining.

We hired a car and set out to meet the doyen darling of the Kerry Cattle Society. Ms. Raymonde Hilliard was the craggiest, feistiest female that one could ever want to meet. Her family had been breeders and exporters of Kerry cattle for over one hundred years and Ms. Hilliard had seen nearly three-quarters of them.

She was driving a giant tractor with a muck spreader in tow. Off-grey splattered dungarees covered a hunched up figure. A very old floppy hat covered half her face.

A PINCH OF SALTEE

"Be with you in a mo", she shouted from inside the tractor's cab as she brought it into her immaculate farmyard. She reversed it, with aplomb, under a covered shed. She alighted from her seat.

"Hello John, and you must be Sir Henry. Welcome. Come in and have a cuppa before looking at the herd". She led us into what can only be described as an unfinished kitchen type room. Very bachelorish. Very masculine. We stood as there was only one chair in evidence. She waffled on with JB giving the odd grunt in reply

After a hurried mug of tea we set sail for the paddocks to view her milking herd. Raymonde out walked us both, JB having a wonky hip remained three strides behind her with me alongside.

My first viewing of her herd created an instant love affair. They were sleek, all jet black and so tame. She knew their pedigrees going back sixty something years.

"That's my best cow over there. She's twelve and she's won many show prizes. Her granddam was also a champion, at the RDS – Spring Show – remember?" questioning me.

"Ah yes, I remember it well."

We spent a good hour with her, amongst her herd, gleaning as much information as possible.

"Michael O'Connor is your best bet, up in the mountains above Lough Carragh near Kilorglin. They'll be real tough heifers – suit your island climate I suggest", was her parting quip.

"I'll phone and warn him you're coming. Best of luck". She hurriedly waved us away. I could feel her orb of intense energy. It generated such passionate rhythms of aspirations. This aura convinced me to travel along 'the Kerry way'.

JB and I moved down the road a mile or two and visited the Muckross Abbey herd of Kerries. They not only had a milking herd but used a Scottish Highland bull to cross for beef purposes. These big shaggy haired Scottish bulls were twice or three times the size of the little 'black divils' as the cows had been described by Ms. Hilliard. Their progeny however, were fine strapping bullocks not unlike buffalos in the distance. We moved down to the Dingle Peninsular next to see what tourism had made of the renowned lone dolphin, Fungi. What we saw was traumatic. It was a rough sea, rain was stair-rodding as we looked out from the Skelligs Hotel where we partook of morning coffee. Throughout this hour of respite we watched the tourist boat attempting to lure Fungi, the dolphin, to the surface. Not even he was interested. We commended him on his appreciation of our Irish climatic conditions!

That night we moved on to the little village of Quin and stayed in a very comfortable B & B. I had to see a man about those useless ewes that had been delivered to me last year, and arrange for their return forthwith. Next day we found the farm of Michael O'Connor and his Oulough herd of Kerries. Michael and two of his sons set off up the hills behind his homestead with JB. I took one look at the terrain and declined politely.

"Can you bring them down nearer to the road please," I asked Michael. JB then spoke of my recent operation with Michael who, very gentlemanly, agreed to my request.

"We will be back within the hour, I'd say, so why don't you go for a drive down that way, you'll get a good view of our Lough Carragh. We'll meet you at that little copse over yonder. See you bye and bye". He had such a soft voice and a wide smile. We warmed to him immediately. These mountainey men were a very special breed.

I took the car around the farm roads and discovered a shimmering little trout lake well above Lough Carragh. Two anglers were casting cool calm waters with wet fly tackle. Within seconds the nearest angler to me had a strike and hooked it. With envy I watched as he played for exactly seven and a half minutes. The brown trout was a whopper – approximately three pounds. I walked across and congratulated him. It was his third. He had been thrashing the water for four hours he told me. Neither of the two had further luck so after another half hour or so I returned to the appointed meeting place. There was a small dam in the field by the copse. A covey of fat wood pigeons escaped from the group of fir trees. The crescendo of flapping wings filled the air like a cloudburst. A single grey heron stalked the still inky waters of the dam.

It was time for my walk so out into the field I went to meet the herdsmen. A rutted bog road lead from the gate gradually climbing up through well grazed lower pastures of the mist enveloped hillside. There was no bracken here but acres of heather. It was too soon for bog cotton to reveal its fluffy symbols. Although overcast it was a serene day, still, save for the odd outburst of bird song. Lark, bunting and blackbird vented their delight. Then I heard, in the distance above me, a 'lowing' call. Cattle were on the move, soon they would give a sighting of canvasses to come. Some of these black beauties would hold sway on our island fiefdom.

And then, there she was. Small, stocky with nostrils flaring. Speckled ivory horns reaching for the stars above a clear pair of frantic eyes. She halted, snorted at me, held me in her rigid stare. I was the intruder on her patch. I didn't dare move a muscle. Two statues from differing worlds stationed themselves head to head. I pictured her on Little Saltee. 'Horny' the lead cow – head of the herd.

Another dozen or fifteen appeared over a wide front. Some gambolling like lambs, others sauntering. They knew they were being driven but little did they know where to. I, a lone human of different hue and aroma, was their focal point. Their heads raised to a new height had nostrils pulsing some pagan smell. They gradually gathered around me forming a circle only ten metres away. The three O'Connors and a rather lame JB formed an outer ring around them.

"Choose the five you want and we'll cut them out of the group", shouted JB.

It took me a good fifteen minutes to build their confidence which allowed me to walk amongst them.

A PINCH OF SALTEE

"O.K.", I called back to them. "The horny one; that one over there grazing, those two side by side here and that little lady, the smallest of them all. Let's see them as a group", I ended.

My walking stick was extra handy, at this juncture, as I not only pointed but guided them away from the rest.

"What about those then?" I asked JB as we neared each other.

"Looks fine to me. But do you really want that horned heifer – she might be a problem".

"I'm afraid I do John. Gut feeling and sentiment rules here. She was the first I saw and all the original breed surely were allowed to keep their horns".

"O.K. then. A good pick I'd say by and large".

He then asked Michael to write down their I.D. numbers from their yellow ear tags. A pen and piece of paper was found in one of the son's inner anorak pockets while the others called out the five identities.

I took one good long final look through the group. I was satisfied. They were my choice. There would be no one else to blame if they didn't pan out. They were now my foundation herd.

Michael, JB and I walked slowly back to the car discussing my chosen five. His sons were driving the rest back up the hill from whence they came.

We sat in the car for a good half an hour discussing the dams[11] of my lot and then we came to the price. JB and I had agreed earlier on the figure that should be offered. We didn't have to make a bid. Michael came straight out with that very figure. I got the immediate impression that any further discussion on price would be fruitless. He said it with such passion:

"That's what they're worth to me and not a penny less I'll accept".

I spat on my hand, he on his and we shook. The deal was sealed.

---

[11] mothers

A PINCH OF SALTEE

On the drive home to his farmhouse we finalised all the veterinary points that had to be taken care of – the movement permits, blood tests and the finding of all their registered papers. I asked if he knew Liam the transporter who had brought the sheep during the previous year and he nodded in the affirmative.

"When the results are through I'll phone him and arrange a date", he said and "come in for the tea now please". He led us in through his kitchen to the front room.

It had been a pleasant day, full of light and shade, beauty and austere mountain magic. I was thrilled with my bevy of Kerry beauties – my five little black 'divils' as Raymonde had so lovingly called them. I relaxed in the knowledge that I had now made the right decision. Kerry cattle would be perfect for the island. It had been quite a hectic day but one full of memories and success.

The following week I phoned Michael to ask how things were going. Blood tests had been taken and at the Mart he had bumped into Liam. He warned him about the impending delivery to me.

"By the way Michael", I enquired, "any chance of those five heifers running with a bull while with you?"

"Oh yes. Right," said he in reply. I could feel the cogs of his brain working overtime, "you'd like them covered if possible would you?"

"I would indeed, Michael. I might get lucky and have one or two calves on the island next year. Would you mind that?"

"No, not at all. Grand idea. As a matter of fact I have a new bull, one of Miss Hilliard's, who will be running with that herd of heifers you saw. I'll put him in straight away then. No trouble at all sir."

"Thanks a lot then. Keep me posted, please," and we both hung up.

They arrived in Kilmore Quay six weeks later. I had to make hurried last minute overnighting arrangements with my builder pal, who had an overgrown grassy acre at the rear of his house, three sides of which were thick thorn and deep ditch. The fourth side had to have wire strung across to contain them. Certainly there was sufficient grass for a week or so. Hopefully we only needed it for a day or two or three! Greg, unfortunately couldn't house them for me at that time.

We were caught by yet another spell of windy wet weather. They had to stay longer than planned. Greg very kindly lent us an electric fence to hold them in. But a Kerry is a Kerry is a Kerry! Never having been in such a confined area before they decided, on the third night, to go look see what Kilmore Quay had to offer. Some irate calls came from neighbours. Out he went with family backup and shooed them with great difficulty back to his little field. They had only been 'out a roving' for a few hours but that was all that proved necessary for one of them to create a hysterical situation some months later.

It was a Thursday. The day dawned windless, calm and dry. Not a cloud in the sky, not a leaf moving in the palm trees adorning most of Kilmore Quay's gardens. I put my phone into overdrive – Greg for trailer and straw, the vet for tranquillising injections, Declan for the metal barge, JB and son David just to be there. Anyone else I could think of to help. This all went on before 8.00am. By 10.00am everyone was in place. The operation had to be run with regimental precision. With lovely amiable Wexford people to deal with, it was a 'doddle'. Lots of onlookers at the Quay side were, however, unable to interpret my loud orders – they obviously thought I was too arrogant. One old dear sidled up to me and enquired:

"What's with you and all the talk? You have the others doing all the work?" My reply was curt but polite:

"Madam, there always has to be a director, its my show. O.K.?"

This received peals of laughter from those who understood the drama of the moment. I should have had cameras, clapperboards, the lot. Then I would have had the authority to yell "lights, sound, cameras, roll!" Only the director's chair was missing.

We had loaded the heifers from the field into Greg's sheep trailer. On arrival at the slipway the vet, Dan Gubbins, injected the two I nominated. He had to estimate how much tranquilliser was needed to allow them to travel out in a happy sleepy relaxed mood and yet 'come alive' when they were off loaded into the sea. This had to be gauged to perfection. Worry had been written all over his kindly face as, at the outset, we discussed the time scale for the voyage. Weight of beast multiplied by minutes gave the volume in c.c. of the dose required. He must get it right. But then, as I found out a little later, he was a true professional.

Straw, donated by Greg, was laid on the bottom of the metal barge. A tarpaulin was placed on the ground between trailer and barge. Once tranquillised their legs gave way under them. They were then hobbled with sash cord. Strong men gently dragged them onto the tarpaulin and across to the barge. More strong men lowered them into the barge placing them side by side on the bottom. Everyone wanted in on the act. We had a full crew.

It was for me the most historic and dramatic moment so far. Cattle being shipped out to the island. It hadn't happened in sixty years.

Declan towed the barge with Tapaidh. Progression was at a snails pace until out of the harbour. We had only loaded two heifers on this first trip. I had to be certain that all my plans were watertight. If this was possible then future trips would be plain sailing.

He took us out on the then calm side of St. Patrick's Bridge, the Carnsore or East side. I lost my beloved old Kenyan farm hat as we left the harbour. A wind had suddenly risen out on the bay. The pace was upped and the barge took a slalom course as we moved from port to starboard at Tapaidh's stern. We got a bruising ride as we crossed back over the bridge near the island.

A PINCH OF SALTEE

A lot of us aboard went a whiter shade of pale but we stuck it out in silence. Two people had been allotted a heifer each. They sat astride or upon their necks. A comfortable bed of straw cushioned the cargo. There wasn't a movement or word amongst us.

Off loading went without a problem. Heifers were untied and lifted gently over the side dropping into the water. Halters attached to a length of rope held by an already wet but sturdy Chris, Rory, David or John would then guide the stock up the rocky shore to pastures new. First trip a total success. And Horny was first to land.

I stayed on the island with JB. We 'shooed' the two displaced looking heifers up onto a good piece of grazing near the homestead. All these heifers were only about four foot in height and were in fine condition with silky black coats.

The second trip with the three remaining heifers luckily also went without a hitch. Probably 'the' most specific item to get right on exports and imports such as this was the tide. We had to have a rising tide as the metal barge had to be kept afloat. On an ebbing tide its weight would get caught on the rocks and wedged.

We drove the last three heifers up the hill to join their friends who already seemed settled. The island was now theirs. They would meet up with the sheep later that evening we presumed. Shirley had not accompanied me on this venture. She felt it was men's work. Men's talk. Men's curses perhaps! I inwardly thought that she probably wouldn't want to witness any hardship to the animals, if anything went wrong.

Once again our village 'office' played host to all those who had helped us through the day. The craic measured storm force eight. Many of the local fishermen, also imbibing there, told me they would keep an eye on my new arrivals. This would prove highly advantageous in the coming years. Another piece of the jigsaw fell into place.

Chapter Five

Divining – First Disaster – New Friends – The Raft – Stock Crush

Having walked the island thoroughly on at least two dozen occasions I outlined the likely under water streams and springs that we were beholden to. I now needed confirmation.

We had found six waterholes – three of these on the eastern side, *Cabots, Shirley's* and *Patrick's* – well defined, some with reeds prominently rooted. The former I named for the international ornithologist David Cabot who visits annually to ring Fulmar, Cormorant and Shag. Man years ago he had planted six Sycamore trees around the area. Some of these, although stunted, remain today. Two more holes were on the southern slope beneath the tallest cairn. The sixth was halfway along the western slopes and was really a quagmire most of the time.

Greg told us about a local diviner, Marty Scallan, and so we went to meet him at his immaculate bungalow a few miles inland from Kilmore Quay. He said he would love to help us. I was, however, worried about his lameness and mentioned this to him.

"Make it a very calm day and I'll be alright," said he in reply. Having been in boats all his life, the wet and damp had now caught up with him, and his hips were giving him hell. I promised I wouldn't attempt to land him until the tide and sea were exactly right. We then talked about his great hobby pheasants, and how he had a good brood of chicks for sale. Showing them to us, I agreed to take them when they were ready.

Some weeks later an ideal day allowed us to bring Sophia right onto the sandy beach area. It wasn't too difficult for Marty to disembark and thread carefully between the rocks to dry land.

He used two pieces of coat hanger wire and spent a good hour divining around the homestead/haggard area. My son Patrick

76

was with us so whenever Marty got a strong 'pull' to earth he instructed Pat to start digging. What we were hoping to locate was the original well which perhaps had been partly filled and covered over with flagstones. Marty was adamant about water being present but, despite half a dozen diggings, nothing was found near the surface.

We left the homestead area and moved up to the central ridge. Along parts of it he got strong indications of an abundance of water, perhaps an underground stream. But not one definite place with signs of water near the surface.

He tried again on returning to the homestead but nothing new raised our hopes. Marty had given us a good three hours of his time but as he said himself "there's plenty of it there but not where you want it like."

It was amazing to see the wires bending downwards with such determination. Marty offered me the chance to try this method. I have a touch of arthritis in my hands and the force I felt was quite incredible. My wrists were completely bent downwards with the force.

"I told you there is water there. A good feeling isn't it?"

"Simply amazing."

I was happy that the island had plenty of springs and underground water which meant stock would be catered for. If necessary I would have to pump from the nearest waterhole to the homestead but that would be in the future.

A second opinion was necessary. I phoned a drilling company in Dublin, explained my predicament and asked their advice. They kindly gave me the contact number of a Jim Burke, a water engineer who they used from time to time. He lived in Dalkey.

We met over the phone and some days later we collected him and spent a day on the island. Jim had been the water engineer in the O.P.W. for many years and had worked all over the country.

A PINCH OF SALTEE

A small wiry man, in retirement, he moved and worked in a precise manner. He had a load of interesting instruments and a magic sphere on a string.

I wasn't getting involved so let him get on with the job in hand. He was receiving a portly fee for his expertise.

Working for an hour or so before lunch and then for a further two to three hours we left again for home, I felt he had earned his stipend.

On the drive back Jim explained his findings. We were blessed with an underground abundance of water distributed in streams from the highest cairn, along the central ridge, with tributaries running mostly eastward. There was, however, a strong underground flow down the hill westward to the haggard crossing beneath the end stall on the eastern building, then across the haggard and below the kitchen.

In this area he recommended we dig the well – say two to three metres from the kitchen door. We should find water at approximately four metres.

During the last three months of that summer Patrick and Liezel were resident on the island. They pitched tent in the second 'open air' cottage. Their main tasks were to dig the well and uncover the cobbled paths of the haggard. Pat took on the arduous well work whilst Liezel discovered cobbles.

Patrick worked his way down six and a half feet before the task became too much for him. The rocks were getting bigger and harder to break making their lifting to the surface too much of a strain. His back was becoming a painful problem. We would have to await a future date for its completion. A great pity I felt.

On their 'off' days, and when stormy weather was forecast, they made their second home at the Kilturk Hostel just outside Kilmore Quay. This building, a converted national school and grounds, was owned by David Sumray who also had an interesting timber business. He imported containers laden with old planks stripped from demolished mills, warehouses and school structures in the deep south of the USA. These he then graded, itemised species wise, and sold on to developers of hotels, pubs, restaurants and the like. In fact wherever architects specified 'olde worlde' refurbishment.

Obviously through this time we all got to know Dave, his partner Jacqui, and their two young children. During one of our nights out together at Quigley's pub in Kilmore, Dave mentioned he had a 23 ft metal boat which he used for pleasure fishing and taking the family out in the bay.

His boat was a splendid yellow creation known to one and all as *the banana boat*. It was significantly longer than Sophia, broad of beam, totally open with three benches, and easily powered by a 15 horse outboard. It would be the ideal backup for our transportation needs. He most generously, offered its use as he only occasionally had the time to spend fishing. *the banana boat* became a very important item in the future of our project.

It was late November and the weather was wet, windy and everywhere was rain-soaked. A roaring fire at home welcomed an evening of reading, writing and t.v. It would be nice not to be disturbed. But Murphy's Law is never far away.

The phone rang in the hall.

"Hello Henry. How's it up there in Dublin?" It was Declan.

"As bad as it is with you I imagine. What can I do you for?"

"Well it's like this," hesitatingly he started off "what do you want first, the good news or the bad?"

"Lets go with the bad. I think I know what you are going to tell me."

"Your new roof is off – that's the bad news. But it's still near the homestead in two or three pieces – that's the good news. Sorry to have to tell you like this."

A PINCH OF SALTEE

I was momentarily silent, remorseful.

"I had half expected it, Dek. Just one of those things I'm' afraid. Thanks for letting us know. We will be down on the next possible calm day. You will take us out, I hope?"

"Yes, of course. Whenever. I won't be taking Tapaidh out of the water 'till February anyhow. Sorry about the roof. Best to Shirley." He rang off.

On returning to our well lived in couch Shirley had already worked out the bad news. She was lovingly stroking Oscar who occupied the third place on the three seater.

"I'm so sorry my darling. But we were half expecting it weren't we, if the storms continued".

"Yes, indeed my love. That blasted builder and his unfinished symphony of sacrilegious cockups." I could have really blown off ...but what the hell!

We knew, from middle September, that this could happen if the storms blew from the west and at persistent force 4 or higher, and they did.

A lot of work had gone into finding the correct finish for the roof. I wanted it to look like tiles but due to the magnitude of the logistics in transporting, hauling and then placing real tiles it was decided by all of us that fabrication would be the answer. The product I chose was Scandinavian in design but manufactured in Navan. I was instructed to order 12ft lengths by the builder. They were delivered to Greg's farm, inspected by the builder, and various locals interested in the project, and then transported out.

The problem was that once erected they were too long and therefore their overhang was approximately 18ins. The builder said he would cut them to lie level with the roof's wall under which a gutter would be placed.

Despite constant pleading from us he never got the job done. My son, Patrick, had assisted the builder in erecting this edifice. It was our pride and joy – the first cottage re-roofed - our residence. I do not like to interfere with artisans who have been contracted to do a job. It is their expertise that I purchase.

Normally I would personally undertake the job and complete it to my own satisfaction. Unfortunately I was not in the health to do it and didn't have the expertise to carry out the work myself.

In hindsight Patrick and I made a mistake. When we realised that our requests were being totally ignored we should have gone to the local hire shop, taken out an angle grinder and cut the overhanging sheets to size. A job that, at most, would have taken us two hours. It was a costly blunder and such a tragedy as the roof had looked so elegant . Now we were to be a year behind in our plans.

The rafters had been blown off their axis and resembled a torment of tangled timber. They too had been incorrectly lodged.

1999 had not been a good year. Its ending, even worse. But, prior to fitting the roof, Patrick and I had painted two coats of varnish onto the pine loft floor which brought out the best timbre in the ton and groove boards. It was to prove a godsend, as despite being open to the elements for the next six months, the loft floor remained in almost perfect order.

We viewed the destruction just before Christmas when two lovely calm days appeared over the horizon. Firstly we found out how really lucky we had been. Storms indeed had done the damage. They had lifted the roof right up and off the rafters. The south half of it had been blown over the entire building and walls on the western side. It was in two pieces and lay halfway down the slope to the shoreline.

The other half (8m x 3.5m) had landed in one piece within the haggard – just 4m from the kitchen/storeroom.

That distance was the difference between total disaster and a lucky let off. If it had landed on the roofs of kitchen/storeroom and bedroom – a total area of 7.5m x 3m – they too would have been demolished and literally everything we had brought out to the island would have been damaged or lost. Someone was looking after us, there was no doubt about it.

A PINCH OF SALTEE

I did let out a few 'f's' and cursed the blaggard who allowed this happen and had let us down. But I had learnt long ago in Africa never to hold grudges. It gets you nowhere.

Both Shirley and I looked at the dumped debris and decided we would pull it apart in the spring and salvage whatever possible. The rafters looked reusable but it would need manly strength to reunite the structure. Not a job we could tackle. Oh well, I mused to myself, 'we lost this one. We will win next time'. That's my philosophy.

We took a walk on the island's wild side. Up there on a granite outcrop it was so tranquil, serene. So much to treasure. I could see white horses schooling over emotive waves as they coursed along a curve of aquatic obstacles. Believe me I said a prayer or three.

Strange how things change, literally overnight, for the better.

The night was December 26 – St. Stephen's Day – we had been watching national hunt racing on television from Kempton Park, England all afternoon.

However, this little episode recounts a chase of a very different kind. I received a phone call from Marty Scallan. He sounded extremely worried and obviously thought I too should be.

He had heard a report that someone had been shooting on the little island that afternoon. The worrying factor was that the cattle and sheep had evidently been seen careering all over the island and he hoped that none of them had been damaged or come to grief over the cliffs.

All this had been told him by a very good friend who was incensed over the situation.

Marty had been putting pheasants out on both islands for years with the understanding that he and another friend could take a bag of them every Boxing Day or thereabouts. He had discussed this arrangement with me and I had fully agreed to it. I had also told a couple of my friends in Kilmore Quay that they too could bag a brace or two in return for keeping an eye on my stock during the winter.

Marty was very upset indeed about the affair and after a good ten minutes of beating about the bush and hedging I managed to get a name out of him as to who it might have been. I promised I would look into the matter immediately.

How best to get to the bottom of this tale I wondered? Greg Stafford came to mind, no better man I told myself. He would have his finger on the pulse and would know who went shooting with whom and where. It had evidently been a lovely dry and calm day down on the Quay.

When I gave Greg the name mentioned by Marty he immediately went on the defensive but nevertheless he would go and see the person. They were close friends.

I received a phone call the following day from Bobby Stafford. He apologised profusely for the upset that I had been caused. He explained, with great passion and insistence, that nothing had happened to frighten the cattle or sheep. Bobby was one of the people I had invited to have a shoot if he felt the urge and the conditions were favourable. This is how he told it. He and a friend had decided to visit the big island as was their tradition on the 26th December of each year. On approaching he noticed another boat already moored off the landing spot. They also heard a number of shots being discharged so knew that a hunting party was already in occupancy. He recognised the boat.

Bobby then decided to move over to our island to see the stock and if anything feathery stirred, discharge a barrel or two. We did not have a large number of mature pheasants. The big island had many more.

He landed near our homestead and shot two cock pheasants. After inspecting the cattle and sheep he gave the homestead a once over before returning to Kilmore Quay.

A PINCH OF SALTEE

Everyone in the harbour knows, not only every boat and everyone else so it wasn't hard for him to work out who was shooting on the big island.

He admitted he should have told me first but as it was only a last minute decision he didn't think I would mind that much. When Greg confronted him with the story of stampeding stock he was both horrified and mortified. His family were farmers and 'never would he put any animal under stress at any time'. That's what he told Greg and reiterated to me over the phone.

I accepted his explanation and said I'd see him soon – not to worry anymore about the incident.

It was only when we returned to Kilmore Quay in the new year that we got to the very bottom of the story.

Bobby was awaiting us down on the quay. He was sitting in his blue lorry. We parked close by.

A tall lean angular lad, late thirties, with long strong arms, he was dressed in faded jeans, hobnailed boots and anorak over shirt and jumper. His greeting involved the 'mother of all handshakes'. He was a strong man who talked in fleeting sentences – some of which I managed to catch; others were completely lost on me. Even at our first brief meeting, some months before, I had noticed the odd 'ef' word creeping in. It was here again - just part of his everyday vocabulary. Some people can pass it off as never having profaned. Bobby was just such a person. I liked his quick fire wit, expressive face, emotive sayings and best of all his confident attitude. He owned and ran a timber business, and his hobbies were shooting and fishing.

I somehow knew there had to be another angle. His explanation proved me correct.

In short, the people shooting on the big island were friends of Marty's and expected to have a great day by bagging birds from both islands. They got unlucky and therefore were furious. Hence the story about the stampeding stock. Jealousy sometimes gets you nowhere.

A PINCH OF SALTEE

Anyhow, the outcome, a happy one at that, was Bobby Stafford became a very great friend and was instrumental in unearthing for us a friendly builder/farmer 'jack of all trades' who assisted in achieving many of my dreams in the next few years.

I had met up with Mickey Strong a few months before when Bobby took me over to his house. Here was a lovely, quietly spoken Wexford farmer. Small in height with the strength of an ox Mickey restores old tractors and mowing machines as a hobby. A family man with sons and daughters he and his wife Jemma had built their bungalow home themselves. The garden was her pride and joy. Perhaps, finally, we were on to a winner. He showed immediate interest in our plans and was 'not backward' in coming forward with bright and colourful suggestions.

"Why pay more", he'd say. I couldn't agree more whole heartedly with him.

I found myself immediately confiding in him. Openness was the answer. My financial cards were placed on the table. We put our heads together and over the next three years we became, not only the best of friends, but involved in a joint farming venture too.

Bobby has a powerful Cobra RIB with a 50 horse power outboard engine. It makes the island in seven minutes! He goes far out beyond and around both islands on his fishing trips. Most evenings, when it is calm and on a rising tide, he will pass close by us, wave, and set off again to relax by spinning his lines for the elusive silver streaks of the deep. He brought Mickey out to us one such evening. Shirley went out to meet them and brought him ashore. Bobby would call back for him in a couple of hours.

We walked the island showing Mickey the stock, water holes, fence and nesting birds. It was his first visit to the island. At the homestead he contemplated the devastation. His comments were brief.

A PINCH OF SALTEE

"That fella should be strung up by the balls and that wouldn't be good enough for him either!" Luckily he didn't know him.

Walking silently through the pieces of roof and rafters, he climbed up onto the loft and surveyed the damage from there. I didn't have to say a word. My thoughts were 'let the master assess it. He'll tell me the best or the worst'.

It was a lovely evening. We finally sat down looking out across the bay to Kilmore Quay. As we sat there lazily playing with a cool Heineken we could have been anywhere in the Mediterranean. A truly fascinating and ever-changing panorama. The bay was calm. Hook Head Lighthouse was flashing its ever constant warning. Boats of all hues and textures idly trawled the silken waters mirrored in front of us.

"Well tell us the worst then", I said.

"I'm just so livid. That anyone could do that to you is just beyond belief".

"It's done, Mickey, it's past, so lets get on with the job in hand".

"O.K. then. I'll need at least two to help put back the rafters. That's a heavy old job – luckily you have the loft to work from. How many ladders have you?"

"One old small one and one good long aluminium one", I replied, "and a steps" as an afterthought.

"That's a start then. I'll bring out all me tools. We need laths for the roof, Bobby can get them, and I'll get you good second hand sheets of heavy gauged corrugated iron. There's no use trying your roofing again – it's dented beyond repair".

"I'll order the perspex panels from the Co-op", I butted in.

"Get the heavy cattle feed-lot ones, they are the best and you'll have plenty of light in there. How are we bringing it all out?"

"Do you know Dave Sumray? He has *the banana boat*. That would bring all we need in one trip".

A PINCH OF SALTEE

"I've met him yes but don't know him well. We say hello to each other. That's about it."

"No problem", I replied as I knew Dave was dying to come out and explore the island with his family.

As both our birthdays are in May we like to throw a joint party for friends and family, usually around about the 20th/25th of the month each year.

One of my oldest friends from Kenya, Charles Lyttle, a retired vet, and I were doing a 'whenwe'. All East Africans are known as this for they invariably start almost every sentence with 'when we were in ---'.

One of the topics we discussed, while having our barbecue in the garden, was rafting down the Tana River which flowed from up near Mount Kenya to the Indian Ocean north of Malindi. This could be a hair raising safari especially when the river was in spate after the long rains.

I recalled my first trip. The raft was a string bag of barrels and bamboo poles lashed together with sisal twine. Expert tribesmen poled us from the calm crocodile infested shallows to the more active centre stream of the milk chocolate muddy waters. There we just drifted at whatever pace was preordained by the flow and force from upstream.

This memory set me thinking and after all our guests had departed I took the sketch pad from Shirley's office. We now had two boats but we were still dependent on Declan's metal barge for heavy freight. How about a raft of our own which could be towed out fully laden and beached at high tide? Pencil was put to paper and a plan using fourteen metal oil drums – seven to a row – sitting in a metal frame of angle iron was devised. On top of this could be a wooden platform. Catamaran in design but not in speed.

A PINCH OF SALTEE

Declan's metal barge was now out of the water awaiting repairs, and this could easily take ages. It would therefore leave us without transportation for heavy building material and the like.

On our next trip to Kilmore Quay I asked a few of my new friends who they thought was the best welder cum metal worker in the district.

I was given a name, George Culleton, 'the best welder in the district' I was told. 'You'll find him in his forge, at his home, if you don't see a big old dirty red panel van down on the Quay'. He evidently did repair work for the fishermen. They then told me where he lived.

George's home was almost next door to the farm that hosts the annual Bannow Rathangan Agricultural Show. His red panel van was parked outside.

A large man was bent over a mass of iron with sparks spewing in a dazzling display that Mr. G. Fawkes would have been proud of! I wandered over to him talking, as I went, to a red setter who affectionately licked my hand craving attention. I could hear the cries of peacocks close by. Suddenly a flock of guinea fowl came racing around a corner of the adjoining barn. Quite a cacophonous greeting. What was to follow I wondered?

Sparks ceased. A welding mask moved to rest above a long red aged face with weeping grey blue eyes. They held me as I moved to greet him.

Introducing myself, I remarked on how busy he seemed to be and complimented him on his peas and guineas. Not a response, just a slight movement of his arm to wipe off the sweat on his face. Not an approach he was obviously used to!

Finally a soft voice emanated from this large dungareed well-worn frame in front of me.

"Are ye the man from the island then?"

"I am that man", I replied hesitantly.

"I've heard of ye". He gave me a discovering look and then his eyes moved to our car behind me. He still held the welding gun in his right hand.

A PINCH OF SALTEE

"Can I help then?"

"Yes please George. May I call you that?"

"You can call me what you like but not early in the morning", and a smile lit up his ruddy face. He put the welder down and wearily moved over to his work bench admonishing the dog as he went. I followed and took out the sketch I had drafted of the raft and placed it on the bench beside him. He surveyed it for a firm three minutes.

"Where will you get me barrels from?" looking me straight in the eye.

"Oh that's easy. Declan Bates has loads and says you can choose whichever you want".

"When do you need this by?"

"Next week if that's ok by you".

Well he gave me a look that withered the very marrow in my bones. His bloodshot eyes suddenly blazed fiery red.

"What's today then"?

"Oh George I was only joking. I won't need it for a month or so – no hurry really". There was a wry smile across his sweaty face.

"Well that's fine then. How about some tea?" he asked, moving out of the workshop. As we walked the short distance to his house I noticed him grimacing every few strides,

"Have you got a back problem George?"

"No – a friggin hernia. At times it really gets to me."

"I know. I've had one removed. They say I'll have to get the other one out sometime too."

"I've been on the hospital waiting list for two and a half years now. They tell me I'll have to wear a corset if it gets any worse."

"Well, I'm ahead of you on that". I lifted up my t-shirt and showed mine. "It's no problem and it does assist, especially in long drives and when lifting things".

"That's what they tell me too. Suppose I'd better get one and wear it. At times the pain is fierce."

89

A PINCH OF SALTEE

Over a grand cuppa in his well appointed kitchen, where the smell of freshly baked bread tickled my nasal buds, my eyes focused on what looked like some exotic bird in his garden.

"I'll show you around before you leave. I collect rare breeds, mostly pheasants – they're from all over the world. Nice hobby it is and relaxing too".

He proceeded to explain the varieties within his collection. Statuesque peacocks strutted their patch, their tails, rainbow eyed, gracing the ground as a bride's train cascades down a cathedral's aisle. The lawn was now invaded by that hungry flock of guinea fowl first seen on my arrival, catching errant grasshoppers and whatever. Their turbo-charged acceleration over short distances is quite extraordinary and fascinating to watch. My favourite recollection of these grey and white bullet-birds was on the Maasai Mara. Hundreds to a flock would warn all other game in the region with their unique squawking cackles if they noted something strange. They are easy to tame and they act, like a gaggle of geese, as superb security officers patrolling ones garden or farm. I immediately wanted some on the island. Their distinctive call would enhance those of our pheasant population.

His large airy pens ran alongside a wind break of tall Leylandia. Variegated greens contrasted beautifully with the myriad of colours exhibited in the plumages on display.

I was amazed by this prism of exotica on show and fascinated by the peaceful respect between man and feathered friend. I could have spent hours just watching this collection which George had put together over a couple of decades. But time was of the moment and I had another pressing appointment.

"What a spectacular collection George. I envy you."

"They're very relaxing and not much trouble you know."

"Can you please come up with a price on the raft. You'll have plenty of time to make it. Oh and by the way, Declan will transport and launch. Great meeting you. See you soon."

A PINCH OF SALTEE

With mixed emotions I moved onto more mundane matters. I thought we had hit it off and I hoped we would have many happy meetings in the future.

Agricultural shows are held every weekend, during the summer months, all around Ireland. Since my return from Africa I had been kept busy commentating at a couple of dozen of these. One such show, and in my opinion one of the best, was the Tinnahely County Wicklow August Bank Holiday event. It is held on the Rothwell home farm which also hosts the annual point-to-point of the Shillelagh Hunt.

Many commercial stands exhibit there and one especially caught my eye. Esmond Engineering, Gorey, County Wexford was showing their wares which included portable pens and feeders for sheep. In conversation with the angular gentleman on duty I enquired whether they could construct a dual purpose crush-pen to handle both sheep and cattle. He became interested when I outlined my raison d'etre and was most emphatic in telling us that 'he would make anything I wished'. In parting we exchanged business cards. We were both taken aback when we read each other's. I was first to speak.

"Are you Grattan Esmond by any chance?" Because in front of me, on the card was Bart G. Esmond. Something some place clicked?

"Yes indeed I am. We must be cousins. We have Grattan Bellews and Grattan Doyles as relatives. Haven't met any of them for years though." He was very matter of fact about it all as we delved briefly into our antecedents. Other farmers were awaiting his attention so I said I would contact him before I needed the crush and once I had taken measurements. We parted with a solid handshake.

Next time on the island I visualised the collecting pen and corral for rounding up the stock. It would be between the old house and the east side of the haggard. The buildings there were much smaller and narrower than on the western side. The first two opened into each other which gave me the idea of housing the crush-pen inside the second stall. It was approximately 4.5 x 2 metres – absolutely ideal for holding four cows or a dozen sheep at a time.

I took precise measurements and sat down to sketch the crush. It would have to be made in Meccano form for ease of transportation and final erection. And who would I get to do that job? Son Patrick was the man – when the time came, I thought to myself.

A tubular pen with gates front and rear. The former embodying a clamp to hold the animal's head firm. Width would be approximately half a metre which would stop any turning around once within the confines of the pen. Four uprights along one side would be embedded in concrete. Two bolts on each gate would roll into clefts in the wall.

This would leave lots of room for the vet and assistants to administer all necessary injections, etc. Oral dosing would be easy when animals could be clamped firmly in one place. After whatever operations or inspections, the animals would then need a holding area which could easily be constructed inside the haggard and running the length of this eastern side. It all sounded so easy – now it had to be constructed and erected. More timber would have to be brought out. I had enough fence posts left over so they would be the uprights for the corral.

I brought the outline sketch of the crush back to Dublin where I worked on it until I had enough information to pass on to Barty. He took the measurements down over the phone and after double checking with me, said he would call on us in Dublin the following week.

His finished plan and price were to my liking so I agreed on the contract. He would deliver it to Mill Road Farm when ready. Also, he would lay it out, against a wall showing me how to assemble it. I thanked him and awaited his call.

First Heifer, Horny at Oulough

A PINCH OF SALTEE

Chapter Six

Botulism – Calves – Demise of Amy Jane –Rafting Out – New Bull - Walls – Shirley's Waterhole

A deathly silence hovered over the island as we landed. Something was very wrong, somewhere somehow. It was eerie. Never had we experienced anything like this before.

From seeing, hearing, smelling the thousands of gulls that flew over and nested on our homestead pastures to the scene of desolation that ravaged each footstep we dared to tread – the place was now a graveyard.

How in God's name had this happened? How had we inherited a pasture of faceless forms – some completely lifeless. Others with necks and heads unable to find the strength to stay erect and alert, lying, as if set by a taxidermist on grassy nests. Single eyes winking blearily as we approached.

Devastation, no, decimation was surely the name of this outrage. But what or who could be the culprit? A pox ridden population of gulls spread out before us. From whence had it arrived?

As Shirley and I departed that square hectare of decay and proceeded, with anger in our hearts, to the other nesting areas I prayed that the scene would not be similar.

Cormorants and Shags, wings akimbo, necks askew, flocked together on eastern cliffs, healthy in number and form. Fulmars soared and glided in fly-past formation. Kittiwake and Razorbill packed sardine-like the southern cliffs. Tense Terns hovered and plunged in death defying dives to the oceans below. A squadron of Gannets, similarly hari-kari like, had found a shoal of sacrificial offerings in the sound between both islands. Most of the major species therefore seemed 'present and correct' Whether or not the burrowing Shearwater and Puffin colonies had been hit by this epidemic would only be determined after darkness, and their return to dry land.

We found dead and dying Herring, Blackback and Lesser Blackback all over the hundred acres. But no place, even came close to the 'dying fields' above the homestead.

It was a gruesome task I had in front of me. The almost dead and dying needed to be put out of their misery. I, therefore, retraced my footsteps, alone this time, and carried out this humane undertaking.

Shirley returned to the homestead and attempted to track down Eugene Wallace (Wild Life Department). Messages were left on his answer phones.

His call came an hour or so later. I had just returned from my dastardly task and recounted to him our findings. My frustration obviously came across in my voice.

"Not a pleasant sight I agree. I'm afraid it's happening all over the county".

"But what on earth is the problem, Eugene?" I needed an answer. The gulls were being put through hell in their lingering death throws.

In a quiet and reserved voice, touched with depression, Eugene answered "well its all down to us humans I'm afraid. It's our black plastic bags of household waste that's the culprit."

"Not on this island," I hurriedly interjected.

"No Henry, you're correct there. It's the dumps – the landfills of Wexford and Waterford. The birds have found them and have gorged themselves on our toxic waste. It's botulism I'm afraid what's doing it."

The line went silent for a moment or two as I gathered my thoughts. Eugene obviously respected my exclamation of horror. He then continued, quite matter of factly,

"Gulls, in particular Henry, have found it easier to make the trip to Dumpsville and partake in our leftovers. They make meals of the waste, fly back to their nests and there regurgitate their recent rancid intake into the mouths of chicks who stomach it without question. Death – a lingering one I'm afraid – is within the next twenty-four hours. That's what has hit your island, not a pretty sight."

"You can say that again and again. Quite ghastly.   And what a shock too for us. Luckily a couple of our sentinels – on the buildings – have so far, escaped the torture."

"This could mean almost total devastation of the species. We will do a count at the end of the summer but be prepared for only a hundred or so couples to be remaining."

"And that's out of …," I butted in.

"The last figure was plus or minus five thousand. Incredible isn't it?"   There was a pause "I'll see you around," and he rang off.

I was aghast at that figure. I know they, the larger breed of seagull, are not the most pleasant to either look at or have around, rather dirty and noisy but no one would wish that chamber of horror on anyone or thing.

Over the next couple of days I gathered up as many of the bodies as I could find, placed them in pyres and set them alight. Ongoing over the next few years we kept finding the odd dozen who had succumbed to that disease. Our gull numbers did crash to below the two hundred mark.

No more were we to witness their crowded attention as, on Oscar's or the cattle's approach, they took off from their peaceful pastures to herald an intruder by circling overhead.

The cattle had learnt to come to my holler – it meant treats in the form of a bucket full of nuts. I would stand beside a knarled old elder trunk, about halfway up the middle of the island and bellow as loud as I could "come, come, come".

Almost immediately, from whichever side, I would notice intense movement in the sky. Gulls had taken off from the path of the oncoming stampede. As soon as the herd reached me, the gulls would then return to the pastures and settle down once again. Neither side desperately upset by the other.

A PINCH OF SALTEE

It also worked another way. If Oscar, in his hunting mode, had taken off well ahead of us, he too would be trigger enough to explode the gulls into flight. This, in turn would signal to the herd that we were present and maybe a snack was on offer.

Horny, God bless her, at a trot would then appear from any of the four corners followed by the others. Very often they would garner the sheep into action and they too would follow to see what the commotion was all about.

By this regular routine we managed to make the herd tame enough to touch – even out in the midst of the bracken and gulls. We all became firm friends. This made them much easier to handle when we wanted the herd down at the homestead.

The inter-action of bird and stock was such a pleasure for us. To be able to walk amongst the Kerries, touching and feeling their skins, noticing that Horny's upright horns had grown appreciably and that her udder was springing again. Rosslea was the next tamest. She refused to extract her head from the bucket, no matter how hard I tried to prise it away. All five of them had individual traits and characters. We bonded with all of them.

From a couple of lobster men came the news that we had 'two calves'. It was music to our ears. These men fished their pots anxiously close to our shores and it was two of them who, the previous year, had offered to keep an eye on our stock. This sighting was a just reward for their vigil. They had informed Greg who immediately phoned us.

Such was the bonus on the original deal. At least two of the heifers had therefore been covered down on Michael O'Connor's farm. Now I wondered if perchance there might be more to come??

At the AGM of the Kerry Cattle Society I had met a breeder, Vincent Collins from Drimoleague, County Cork. Ms. Hilliard had advised me that Vincent had a grand two year old bull for sale and that it would be ideal for my foundation herd. A couple of drinks 'aprés meeting' sealed the deal so the very next day I contacted JB to relay my good fortune.

He agreed to accompanying me and would lend me his trailer and pickup. Some weeks later we drove to County Cork, found the Collins farm, unhitched the trailer and went to find a B & B. That evening we drove to the busy fishing port of Castletownbere taking a strolling look at harbour, fleet and quaint little streets and shops. A much larger version of Kilmore Quay.

Next morning we collected Knockane Uinseánn, walked him into the trailer and set off for Kilmore Quay.

We stopped at various places along the way for coffees and lunch, arriving at Greg's Mill Road Farm early evening. It had been an eventless journey – even aboard the ferry boat at Passage East coming from Waterford to Wexford.

Uinsean had settled into an abundantly laden straw bed and had remained lying down for the entire trip. He seemed to have a pleasant facile character and he was hornless. At Greg's he was stabled in one of the thoroughbred boxes. He ate his nuts, hay and drank a bucket of water. He was totally laid back.

Now he awaited 'perfect conditions' being posted on the weather front for his future stud duties.

A really amusing incident occurred whilst Patrick and Liezel were resident on the island on their own at this time.

He phoned to ask about the colour of Kerry calves.

"Are they always black Dad – like our first two"

"Yes, unless they are crossbred – why?"

"Well we have been missing one cow, Oulough Birch, for the past few days and today I found her with a big udder – as if she had calved."

"That's great news" I blurted in as it meant we now had three out of five in calf "but what seems to be the problem?" I hastily added.

A PINCH OF SALTEE

"Well, we have just returned from a recce, watching Birch return to a very thick part of the bracken above *Shirley's* and settle down out of our sight."

"Yes, go on."

"Well we traced her tracks and found her with a gorgeous cream heifer calf. Cream all over Dad – not a sign of black anywhere!"

"Wow – that is strange. I guess an opportunist from the next door farm in Kerry must have paid her a visit?" We both laughed our heads off.

"She's really strong and gorgeous. Any ideas on how the others will treat her. Will they accept her? You know how timid Birch is already. This will give her a greater complex."

We joked about it for a good few minutes before I concluded with "keep your eyes on her for the next week anyhow and tell me when they are back in the herd proper. Hopefully we will be down in the next week, once I have all my medical tests approved. Well found – oh, bye the bye, any signs of water?"

"No – afraid not. Only boulders and they are damn heavy. Cheers." We signed off. I pondered our latest and most interesting arrival.

That night I phoned Ms. Hilliard and asked about genetic throwbacks. She was horrified and said it had to be a 'mistake'. I left it at that for the time being.

When next in Kilmore Quay I quizzed our original builder about the time the five heifers had broken out and how far had they roamed? He gave me an unsatisfactory reply as he didn't know exactly where they had wandered to.

On questioning Greg about what farm in the close neighbourhood of the builder's house, had what cattle I learnt there was a herd of Charolais quite close to him.

"They could have visited them, " he said with jollity in his tone.

"Well, I think you have solved the riddle then," says I as I went on to tell him about our latest foundling.

99

"Should be a right good mix that. You can keep her as your house cow."

We both were much amused by this. He ended by saying "Can't wait to see her".

It was quite an amazing piece of timing if in fact my theory was true. Their escape from their fenced paddock and the fact that Oulough Birch was in season. She must have lead the breakout and hightailed it to the bull!!

The calf could not be registered as a pure Kerry but she would be an extra suckler cow for the future. She was christened Buttercup by Shirley.

During this same period the project suffered its first loss. The demise of Amy Jane, our tiny orange inflatable. It took everybody by surprise but left the Patrick and Liezel without a dinghy. There was Sophia out on the mooring – tantalising close but ever so far in reality.

Fate once again showed its hand. We had bought a cell phone immediately on returning from South Africa after my heart attack. It was primarily for use on the island. Now it made its first emergency call. We had left it out with Patrick whilst we returned to Dublin.

"I'm afraid I have bad news. Amy Jane has blown up and the bottom has been severed from the tubes." A chastened son started to pour out his emotions "I don't exactly know what why or how it happened. We just found it in pieces when we went down to have a dip. We hadn't heard any explosion so were not expecting anything unusual."

I jumped into the conversation with "had it been a hot day?" If left fully inflated on very hot days we had been told that the tubes could expand and explode.

"Yes, quite – we were sweating like stuffed pigs. That's why we decided on a swim. Any ideas about what's to be done next?"

"Well we will try and buy another as soon as possible. How are rations with you then? Can you last out for a couple of days?"

"Oh yes – no problem there and the weather is sensational – no storms in sight so Sophia is safe at her mooring."

"OK. Leave it with me and we'll be back to you at lunchtime tomorrow." I hastily added – "any sign of water yet?" alluding to his digging of the well. "No, lots of stones, some big buggers too." I felt almost bitterness in his tone. "OK then, keep well, we'll be in touch."

It was 4.00pm so I got on the phone to all the marine outlets we knew – Western, Killen and Green – enquiring about new and second hand inflatables. We had decided they were the best modes of transport for us.

Bob Killen lent us a 4 metre second hand Yamaha with a semi rigid bottom (Amy Jane had a soft one) to try out. It was the same price as a new 3.5 metre non-rigid.

We took it down next day to the slipway but found it too much trouble to put together and take apart – and it was almost twice as heavy as Amy Jane. It looked about twice her size too.

Declan took us out and we rowed the inflatable into a relieved duo of modern day castaways.

Pat liked the look of the dinghy but we felt it was too big and heavy for us – the old ones in the equation. We had brought out plenty of fresh supplies for them.

During the few hours we spent out there we walked the island and inspected the stock, checked the water holes and peered down the well hole. Not an easy job but one that needed a time scale to achieve anything.

I tried to explain to Patrick that all that was needed to get to a depth of twelve feet was a daily dig of six inches. He could then complete the distance within a month. It meant that he would have plenty of time for fishing, bird watching and any other farm chores that needed to be seen to.

A PINCH OF SALTEE

Liezel was making great progress with unearthing the cobbles. She was also discovering all the original Blue Bangor tiles that had been taken off the roofs in the 1940's when all roofed buildings were being taxed. When our last tenants departed the farm they left all buildings roofless, with the well at the homestead closed in. As yet undiscovered.

Declan picked us up later in the afternoon. Returning to Dublin that evening we left back the borrowed inflatable next morning and bought a spanking brand new 2.5 meter grey Yamaha from Bob Killen and drove back to Kilmore Quay that afternoon.

We phoned to tell Patrick the news and to expect us on Declan's 4.00pm run. Hopefully we would be staying for as long as the good weather held. The dinghy remains with us today.

I had become an addict to the pages of Ireland's twice weekly 'Buy and Sell' newspaper. Such a dictionary of delights within its covers.

Once we had installed a towing hitch to the car, our quest then was for a suitable little all purpose trailer. Every trip to the Quay had the back seat of the car jam packed full of this and that. In everything we purchased we had to be confident that it was completely manageable by our aging bodies. Nothing must be heavy or difficult to carry or manipulate. Some things, however, did fall into that category.

After half a dozen false alarms – either too heavy, too decrepit, too frail or too expensive, one advertisement finally, from someone out near the airport, sounded as if it could be the ideal thing.

We travelled out one afternoon and found the address quite easily. A charming man, an ex scout master, showed us a little yellow and blue painted trailer with a canvass cover. It had a spare wheel and the timbers seemed in good repair as was the tow hitch. The best factor, however, was its weight – easily manoeuvrable by both of us.

A PINCH OF SALTEE

I haggled a little over the price and got it down to my figure. It was a sturdy little item as it had been used to transport tents and equipment for the local scouting troop. We hitched it up and drove off into a sky reddening for the night. Over the next number of years its value appreciated a thousand fold carrying such diverse commodities as cement, engines, sheep, hay, furniture, food, building materials et al. An absolute gem of a workhorse.

The tools of our trade were now in place – boat, dinghy and trailer.

Following this latest purchase I put my imagination into motion and came up with one really bright idea which actually worked. It became a masterly tool in assisting in the chore of transporting all items up to the homestead. I designed a stretcher – two wooden dowels, 2m long, inserted into a canvas rectangle of 1.8m x 1m. This enabled us to carry most of our loads more evenly up the shore.

This was also how we humped the lambs and old ewes down to the water's edge prior to transporting them to the mainland for butchering. It was also used to carry up bales of hay, sometimes three at a time.

I had already warned Patrick, who was now working in Dublin, to be ready for a weekend's 'fun' so he wasn't surprised when I called to make plans. The crush and the bull were at Mill Road and the weather for the weekend looked promising. The day of the big launch dawned bright, blue and the outlook was calm. Bull, timber, roofing sheets and crush – a good two and a half tons of freight.

Dan came down to the slipway and injected Uinseánn, the bull.

A PINCH OF SALTEE

Declan brought the raft to the loading area and attached it to Tapaidh. Timber and roofing came with Bobby.

We loaded a well tranquilized Uinseánn – all ton and a half of him – onto the raft. He was hobble tied as well. He took up the rear half of one side of the raft. In front of him we loaded the nine elements of the metal crush. Along side both of them went all the timber and above them we loaded the roofing. This lay on a platform I had George make in case I wished to house animals in a standing position.

It was my very own 'Kontiki' invention. I prayed it would work as we didn't have enough time to really test its capability for weight carrying! It floated perfectly...?

When all was loaded, a couple of helpers, Patrick and Rory Stafford, stayed on the raft. The others went up front on Tapaidh with Declan.

The cortège slowly slipped out of the marina into open water. Shirley and I, in Sophia, acted as outriders.

Declan took it slowly – the sea was calm and it wasn't too warm a day. About halfway across we noticed a fog spreading out from the big island towards us. We closed across to Tapaidh's starboard bow and remained with her until about 400 metres out from our mooring. We then sped ahead, tied up Sophia, and jumped into the inflatable.

He brought Tapaidh in as close to the shoreline as possible where we then took a length of rope I had left on the raft and dragged it to the shore. I landed, keeping a grip of the rope, and bound it around a tall rocky outcrop. Shirley tied up the dinghy, out of the way of the oncoming raft. Meantime the lads had moved from Tapaidh to join the two on the raft while Declan moored alongside Sophia.

They poled the raft in by using some of the timbers stacked aboard. It was a rising tide, about two hours before high.

Uinseánn was dozing peacefully but not totally out for the count. Once the raft was up to the sandy area everyone got to work untying and offloading the freight.

A PINCH OF SALTEE

The bull, once free but halter tied to a lengthy piece of rope, now in my hands, came to life in a lost dozey sort of way. He splashed over into the sea about waist high and let out a loud bellow. He just stood there contemplating. Three people were allotted to guide him up over the rocks which that day housed an evil smelling rancid spread of seaweed. I still held the lead rope – quite what I should do if he took off and careered over the skyline, I didn't know – but hope and optimism reigns eternal with me.

After a good thirty minutes of huff, puff and cajole we managed to put him into the small stall where the crush would be erected. A bucket of water, some beef nuts and hay was provided for his B & B. Patrick was invited to keep an eye on him whilst the others carried the freight up to the homestead area.

Shirley had brewed up tea, coffee and made a pan of 'hangsandwiches'. These were demolished in seconds. It was then time for the lads to pole the raft back out to Tapaidh with a 'home Declan and don't spare the horse power!' It was a job well done. And the raft had worked. Hail George Culleton and all who travelled on her. Another piece of the jigsaw fell into place.

But that wasn't the end of this little saga. We were all pretty exhausted so turned in early after a spicy 'braai'.[12] It was 4.30am when Shirley and I awoke to the sound of a gate being torn down and hooves heavily pounding the ground outside our bedroom. We looked out the pigeonhole of a window to see Uinseánn staggering across the haggard with a gate in tow. I screamed for Patrick to wake up – he was in a tent 30 metres away – which he did. We all put on some clothes, whatever was nearest and easiest to find, and raced after the bull who was now heading down to the shore.

Luckily the gate had become untangled but the long rope was still attached to the bull's halter.

We caught hold of the rope and actually stopped him, brought him to a halt on his hopeful escape route. I certainly

_____
[12] Barbecue – South African word

didn't fancy swimming after him if he decided to return to the mainland. Patrick and I got to his head and each took a side of the halter. Shirley careered over the headland and got ahead of him down on the shore. She grabbed by him tail.

Uinseánn hadn't a clue as to his whereabouts and looked extremely perplexed. He had a nice nature – nothing ferocious in his makeup as had been borne out by his travels with me since JB and I had first seen him.

We managed to turn him around and once facing back up to the homestead he eased quite readily to our guiding. As we brought him up the path Shirley suggested we take him straight up to the cows there and then. She went off to get a bucket of nuts as Patrick and I guided him up the hill.

The dawn was breaking and stars were fading. Shirley's strimmed path cut a clear swathe through the bracken. We followed it. She joined us about halfway up the hill. She offered Uinseánn the nuts. He refused. After a short rest for all of us she returned to his rear end and whacked the bucket against his bottom when we couldn't get him to move.

Well, if any of you have witnessed a blast off at Cape Kennedy this was another. My arms nearly left their sockets and I dropped the rope and halter. Patrick held on, striding like a gazelle through the bracken, after an explosive bovine missile. Then I watched open mouthed as I saw him fall headlong into the thick undergrowth – he still held the rope and was dragged a further 200 metres before the bull came to a stop, snorting incessantly. He was tired too.

I ran as best I could to Patrick who came to his feet but without his glasses. He was a total stranger in this light – naked without glasses. He had worn them for fifteen years.

There wasn't time to look for them at that moment as 'you know who' started to move again. This time he chose to go upwards and towards the pathway that lead to his, about to be surprised, harem. In one way we all breathed a sigh of relief.

A PINCH OF SALTEE

The area that Patrick's glasses had been pulled off would surely be easy to find again – the bracken was well trampled all around.

It didn't take us long to find the herd of startled heifers. They, most likely, were awakened from their south coast slumbers by all the noise we had been creating. They were moving from the southern section into the northern when we saw them.

Uinseánn liked what he saw and took off at a good steady trot. Patrick kept with him and once the animals met up it was easy for him to slip off the rope from the halter. The heifers seemed pleased to have a male in their midst. They soon took him away from us and returned to their favoured southern fertile pastures.

We set about searching for Patrick's glasses by tracing the events of the previous forty-five minutes. It was nearly 6.00am and that lovely early pastoral light allowed us privy to places recently undiscovered in the midst of the murky morn.

"Needles in hay stacks" was much on our minds as doggedly we retraced every footstep and drag path mowed through the dew splattered bracken. The curse of the island!

"I've got em" shouted Patrick as his hands touched a familiar frame amongst a clump of ragwort stalks. Shirley and I were looking, Pat was feeling. His touch won the race of recognition. Once again he became the son I knew of old. Quite amazing what a pair of glasses does to a face.

"As a matter of interest," I queried "do you have a spare pair?"

"No Dad, I don't I'm afraid. Rather stupid really."

"I'll agree to that alright. Please get yourself tested again soon – even buy a pair of these cheap magnifying ones on sale everywhere now. I have at least two pairs of them in case of accidents."

"Yeah, yeah, that's an idea Dad." And that's a reply I knew so well. It meant nothing would be done.

Both Shirley and I thanked him profusely for his stalwart effort in such adversity. His arms and legs were horribly scratched and smarting from nettle stings. Both he and I only wear shorts and t-shirts on the island – a throwback from our African bush upbringing I suppose. It could be painful, but that wears off in no time at all I had found.

Whilst Shirley made tea we went down and soaked our limbs in sea water, rubbing ionized smelling fresh seaweed into all the searing regions. Within minutes these sensations eased. Whilst Patrick and I were cooling our cuts, Shirley had changed into shorts and t-shirt as the day was hotting up. She met us on her way down to the seashore to do exactly what we had just completed.

I noticed her legs were a mass of cuts, bruises and blood blisters. Not a pretty sight I remarked. "How on earth did you get all those?"

"Oh you know here and there. Remember when the bull was making his way down to the shore, well I rushed over that mound there and literally slipped lengthways all the way down to the rocks. Most of them must have happened then. You know me – the slightest bump and I bruise."

"Get those legs and arms into the sea – rub them with seaweed and that will stop the irritation. I'll get breakfast ready for you."

She returned ten minutes later. The bleeding had subsided but her arms and legs really did look a right mess. With a great big smile she said "Nothing hurts, just looks terrible."

The remainder of that day was spent with Pat and me digging holes, mixing cement, erecting the stock crush. It fitted just perfectly. We found stones, however, in the wall where the bolts were meant to fit and this caused us problems in shutting the gates. In the end we engineered a compromise. We hoped it would hold when the weight of the animals tested it.

Shirley spent most of her day restoring the wall that ran up and away from the crush. She found that fifty years, and maybe more, of weather changes had moved soil and stone up to and over parts of the once perfectly formed obstacle. She would dig – with the African Jembe – alongside the wall, revealing stones of all sizes that had become dislodged from their original placing. These would then be lifted to fill gaps and increase the height of the wall.

One of the items in our REPS Plan is to restore and conserve stone walls. If we had hedge rows on the farm they too would be targeted.

Basically it is to do with ecology and endeavouring to restore and retain boundary fences for the good of the environment. In our plan we highlighted the stone wall running up, from within the haggard, over the hill and joining up at a gateway with two other walls.

The hardest part, and the task that took almost the first two years of our precious time, was the reclamation of the 20 metres within the haggard. This wall had been totally demolished and stones lay strewn over a very wide area. It was the dividing north wall and joined onto the eastern buildings. These we were making into the holding and crush pens.

We built up this wall to almost 2 metres. Some very large stones formed part of its renovation. We were assisted in this by literally every visitor who graced our shores. They were very generous with their strength and time.

Once this was up it made a fine wind break for the garden and picnic area within the haggard. We then brought out a picnic table with side benches to seat six. It was made by Moore's Barn in Kilmore Quay.

On the north side of the wall I constructed a wooden 'boma' – a fenced quadrangle with ancient hardwood marine planks (washed up on our shores) as seats. Inside Patrick constructed our braai. I made the sides high enough to stop the wind but low enough to see over and out onto the bay. We used old lobster pots as bases for tables. Within its confines we appreciated the warmth and intimacy of many a grand gathering.

A PINCH OF SALTEE

Beside it we built up the three sides of another wall which one day when roofed, I thought would become our tractor shed.

From the eastern buildings the old dilapidated wall ran steeply up the hill in an easterly direction. On its south side there would have been a drainage ditch, now filled in. The restoration of a wall, therefore, not only requires its height to be rebuilt but its surrounds re-established.

Prior to my heart attack we both worked on it. This would take up a few hours a day between the other necessary chores.

After the attack it became Shirley's domain. She was assisted occasionally by family and visitors in upending and carrying stones back to and replacing them correctly on her cleaned and remodelled masterpiece.

Oscar would never be far from her and would appear from beneath the bracken every twenty minutes or so covered in dirt. He would be digging 'to Australia', as I put it, after a fast bunny that got away!

I would most probably be cleaning up the garden – not quite as strenuous as Shirley's work – when he would appear, show himself off and partake in a long cool drink from his bowl over beside the bath. Sometimes, if he looked really hot and exhausted, I would take him down to have a swim. He absolutely adored this pastime. He was a strong and confident swimmer. He hadn't yet, unfortunately, become a fisherdog!

I had brought from South Africa some day-on-day agricultural tools. Items that were used by one and all in both Africa and Asia – like the jembe. This, to all intents and purposes, is a hoe, but it is used, as a spade, to till land, harrow and then prepare for planting.

Many a 'tenner' have I won in betting someone of European extraction that I could open up a given patch of ground faster than he could with his chosen implement – a spade perhaps?

I brought back two kinds of these tools. The other was a heavier model but more like our Irish mattock.

A PINCH OF SALTEE

Shirley found both of them a godsend on her never ending wall of restoration. Some of the stones had been blown off, away from the wall, and then buried beneath the sands of time – even up to a metre from their original placement. These had to be dug out, sized and then replaced on the remaining stones to build its height.

Rabbits had burrowed beside and beneath the wall making footholds unsteady and quite dangerous. Far too easy to sprain an ankle in these conditions. Shirley understood these pitfalls and worked steadily away, on both sides, completing a few metres each time. It would be a long arduous task but a rewarding one. We only had such short stints of precious time to fulfil these sorts of tasks. Farming was not a twelve month affair out on this island. We wished it could be but age, weather and income determined the length of time spent out there.

One of these rewards was the day we brought out some guests. From far off our mooring two of them blurted out, virtually in unison, "what's that lovely defined line running up the hill?" I was proud and happy to let Shirley reply, quite matter of factly, "oh, that's the wall I've been restoring."

"Gosh, it looks magnificent, well done."

"You will see it close up very shortly now."

"If we can help in any way just say. I am sure you could do with a little help at times."

This prompted me to respond with, "you bet you're life on that. She won't allow me near it. She says I'm under doctor's orders. I say poppycock and utter twaddle – but have to obey 'she who rules'." We all laughed.

The next reward came in the form of a truly magnificent enlarged photograph of her wall taken at bluebell time by a local artist. Willie and his wife Anya live, for a major part of the year, in Kilmore Quay. The rest is spent in his native Germany. In retirement his two passions are art and sailing. So what better place to settle in than Kilmore Quay, on a piece of prime real estate sold to him by Greg Stafford. This exquisite piece of land is next to a beach on the east side of the harbour, almost at the start of St. Patrick's Bridge. They have the most beautiful views of the islands and both bays. Willie displays his artistic 'oils' in the Upper Deck Restaurant.

As well as owning a grand ketch they also have a large RIB powered by two enormous outboard engines.

One lovely afternoon they landed on the island unbeknownst to us, and despite looking and walking a fair old way around the farm, could not locate us. We were both happily working at *Shirley's* which is hidden in a hollow on the east side.

However, being good neighbours, they left a fine bottle of Valpolichella on our bay table – without a note? When we returned later that evening we both noticed the bottle but did not remark on it. We each thought the other had put it out ready for the evening meal.

Only when we quizzed each other after I had opened it did we realise that it was a present from some good but unknown visitor. I had a suspicion as to who the donor was.

After much discussion I decided to phone Greg and Philomena and ask them if by chance, they knew whether Willie had been out to us.

"Oh yes," said Philomena, "they told us they would take a trip out to you if it was calm enough to land by themselves." Willie had recently landed both Greg and Philomena on the island.

"Well that solves the question then," and I told her about the mysterious bottle of vino.

Some days later we bumped into Willie and Anya on the marina and questioned them,

"Yes, it vas us but vee couldn't fine you to join with us in a bottle so vee left it for you. Hope you enjoyed it. Oh, by the vay I took some photos and ve vill let you have them ven developed."

As I said before – nice to have neighbours like them. Three of these photos are framed and adorn our hall at home.

A PINCH OF SALTEE

Shirley's other major project was her waterhole. I like to give names to places as it makes it so much easier to describe. Hence the three waterholes are *Shirley's, Patrick's* and *Cabot's.*

Hers was the first we opened up and enlarged. From all the artefacts found in and around – spades, horse shoes, kettles, etc. – it was obviously the outlet most used when the tenants farmed the land.

The African jembe came into its own here as one could place it in the water, touch the muddy bottom and drag a head of soil back out onto dry land. All this could be done with one strong movement. Very good exercise for arms and shoulders. Shirley became extremely adept at it. But I made her promise to only work for short spells as it was too exhausting a task. I think she mostly followed my request.

As it was such a good spring we decided to bring out four large pvc tanks each holding 1000 litres of liquid. These would be filled in the rainy season when so much water was evident over the island.

These containers were used for importing medical products, the fluid used in drips in hospitals. They came from the USA. Enclosed by a metal grid they were attached to a wooden pallet. This made it easy to transport. Once the liquid had been decanted the unit was then sold on to traders. It was from one of these that I purchased our first four tanks.

I asked him to disentangle them from the cage and pallet. They therefore became light and manageable – although still very bulky.

I wished to have them in tandem and to fill and empty as one from the other. To do this I got a plumber to drill a hole at the bottom side of each tank and to fit a copper pipe with washers. These could then be joined by a flexible tube to each other. The end tank would be fitted with a locking tap on its exit pipe. From there another flexible pipe would take the water to whatever receptacle I decided upon.

A PINCH OF SALTEE

Each tank could be filled from the top. But, with this method, only one needed to have the water fed into it. All tanks, if level with the others, would then fill up automatically to the same level at the same time.

Taking them out to the island presented no problem as we loaded them on to Tapaidh when Declan had a trip to the big island.

The next bit was the tricky test. We off loaded them all onto Sophia at our mooring much to the amusement and amazement of the tourists aboard Tapaidh. Poor Sophia was swamped by these enormous amorphous containers strung together with a length of rope. My one regret was I had no camera. One of the tourists did take some shots – but as yet nothing has appeared.

Luckily the sea was calm. Somewhere amongst them, and up on the cuddy, Shirley could see the route in. I certainly couldn't. I cut engine and glided in the last twenty metres up onto a bed of kelp. Shirley jumped into the water grabbing the bowline whilst I pulled up the engine.

We then off loaded them onto the kelp and rocks. It was a receding tide so they were safe. All we had to do was return Sophia to the mooring, tranship and ride back in the dinghy. So easy to write about but quite a chore in reality.

The tanks were then carried up by us to the homestead, once the dinghy had been put to bed. We needed a drink – a very long drink.

Next morning we carried them, one at a time, on the stretcher, across the three-quarter of a kilometre to *Shirley's*. That afternoon we placed them on a platform of planks, joined the pipes and filled them from the pool. The distribution of water was carried out by our little bilge pump working off a twelve volt battery. This was the first time we had tried the unit, an idea we both thought would have plenty of use on the island. Our gut feeling had succeeded once again.

A PINCH OF SALTEE

We then had four thousand litres of water as standby. A very worthwhile conservation project was now in reserve. Another piece of the jigsaw was in place.

Watertanks at *Shirleys*.

A PINCH OF SALTEE

Chapter Seven

Making Ready – Shearing – Guests – Stock Over Cliffs –
The Cabot Connection

Whenever we arrive at Kilmore Quay to visit the island farm it is not just a matter of climbing into Sophia, pressing a button and off we go. One day, please God, it will be just like that. But for the first five years the routine went like this.

First hurdle is to open the marina gate. This is quite the nastiest and heaviest hinged gateway we have ever come across. It is on a slope which makes it difficult to open and pass through while burdened with baggage. It takes the two of us to operate it – one to hold it open, the other to carry things through. It becomes even more difficult and maddening on our return trips as we are this time laden with black rubbish bags, cool boxes, clothing, etc., etc. And probably a lot more tired and weaker than when we set out.

Security demands that special keys and locks are only issued to those renting berths in the marina. Kilmore Quay has a harbour master, Captain Eddie Barrett, and two assistants, Johnnie Synnott and Peter Devereux. The latter two are kept immensely busy during the hectic summer months when visiting yachts overnight and stay for short periods. Their berthing fees have to be promptly collected as sometimes berthing facilities are not that easy to allocate. This is due to the volume of navigable traffic - a definite growth leisure pastime with enormous investment. Security is top of their list in protecting everyone within the marina. The gate, therefore, must be kept locked at all times.

Lady Sophia's berth is just to the port side of the entrance walkway. Once we have offloaded all the baggage from the car and trailer, carried it down to the berth and deposited it beside Sophia, we then undress her ladyship!!

116

Tony, Shirley's eldest son, and his two sons, Alex (14) and Matthew (9) stay over the August Bank Holiday weekend on an annual visit. Sometimes this coincided with my son Patrick's presence. Such an opportunity could not be missed. Sheep shearing became the task for one of the days.

After breakfast all of us would walk the island, find the flock and drive them back to base. We would be accompanied by Oscar and Crunchie, the Nicholson family's spunky Yorkie type terrier.

The first season we drove the sheep into one of the cottage ruins. These have very high walls and two open doorways. One of these we managed to close off with corrugated sheeting. The other had a human, hopefully to block the exit. Armed with a barrel as shield and a hefty stick the blockade worked.

Having no power (generator) in those days, we had to use hand shearers – the large scissor action type and it was a mighty long time since I had last attempted this in Kenya. However, I started off by showing both Tony and Patrick how it was done.

One shaggy ewe was caught by grabbing a hind leg and holding fast. Then either of the sons picked her up by grabbing the wool below the neck and plonking her onto her bottom between his legs. The other son would then commence shearing down the belly line through to the back. We would shear in relays until the whole fleece fell off. Shirley would join the shearing duo when one of the men started squawking about 'his back was killing him'. She would then finish off, without a word said, where they had given in! I would then cut and doctor their feet. There is a special secateur like tool for this. Some hooves would be completely overgrown so a lot of pruning took place. Rather like getting stuck into the favourite rose bush and pruning it back to a few inches above the main root stem.

Last thing before release was to give each one a further dose of liver fluke remedy, either by injection or oral dose.

Then we would catch the next and so on, until all the ewes and rams were bereft of their woolly jumpers.

Bail out the rainwater – if it has rained since our last trip – then offload the inflatable and its engine. Place these on the jetty, unpack the inflatable and pump it up, Shirley usually has this chore whilst I carry the outboard to wherever we can find a spot to launch the dinghy. Oscar meantime is hunting the shoals of mullet that tantalise and tease him by dipping under the next boat and then the next and the next and so on. Some of them are immense – all of 3 to 4 kilos. They know him well and also have learnt that he is disciplined not to jump in after them. So a great game actively unfolds in this regular theatre of pisces versus caninus! He knows when to board Sophia – the exact moment when Shirley unleashes the bow and stern lines and I get set to pull our 15 hp Evinrude into life – hopefully! It usually starts on the third pull but sometimes like Murphy's Law, it takes up to three minutes. Many curses, a rising BP and attempts by Shirley not to placate me, but to add the feminine touch to my macho engine, and mostly with success!

She knows her dinghy's engine, a 4hp Yamaha, like the back of her hand, and I, usually, handle mine with alacrity.

Once loaded and started, with dinghy and outboard in tow, it takes fifteen to twenty minutes to reach our mooring off the island. Sometimes it is calm, sometimes not. When it is the latter we crash over, up and down the western rollers – a sensation and noise that Oscar does not appreciate. He cuddles up close to Shirley, sitting just in front of the cuddy, and hates the banging of fibreglass against water.

At the mooring I slow down and attempt to glide onto the buoy. Shirley is now up on the bow with a long hook ready to catch the rope. Currents are strong in this vicinity. If the sea is rough she will have clambered over or alongside the cuddy gripping a rope strung from bowsprit to the bench she and Oscar had been sitting on.

Shirley is dead eyed and has an almost perfect hundred percent score at this tricky manoeuvre. She then has to hold onto the loop of the buoy and place it over the bow cleat and tie it tight.

I then rope in the dinghy and bring her alongside attaching her ropes aft and stern. I cut my engine, lift it out of vertical into a 45 degree position enclosing it with a canvas cover.

We then discuss the freight and how many trips we need to land it all on the shoreline approximately 100 metres away. Usually the first load will be the three of us with as much of the heavy and awkward items as is possible. This is governed by the calmness, or otherwise, of the sea at this juncture.

Both paddles on the dinghy are put into places of readiness for they are vital in guiding us in over the last 20 to 30 metres. Oscar is mad keen to plunge in and get ashore so that he can charge up onto the grassy foreland and catch a bunny or two napping.

He is given the go ahead in the last 10 metres as I prepare to off load myself into cold sea and kelp. I guide the inflatable by towing her onto the shore. I am usually dressed in shorts and sandals.

Shirley then hands me the baggage and I place it on the rocks 20 or 30 metres inland. Once all is unloaded we then dismantle the engine and carry it up over the rocks to dry land. We then return for the dinghy and carry her up the same route.

Shirley may have to make two or even three trips back out to Sophia to collect the rest of the cargo before we put the dinghy to bed. That means, slightly deflate it, check all items, life jackets, bailer and sponge, pump, ropes – which are then stored inside it before covering with a blue plastic sheet to save its skin from the heat. The cover has then to be battened down with small rocks to hold it in place in case high winds should prevail.

Then we return to the load and carry it up, piece by piece, to the homestead.

Meantime Oscar will have spent that half hour or more exploring everywhere around the homestead, hopefully having caught a rabbit or two that were unprepared for his arrival. Although I have fenced in this area with chicken wire, errant rabbits seem to be able to penetrate the defences at will. I am

118

positive they have an underground tunnel from the wall o through the inner wall and can 'pop in' whenever we ar resident. All to the detriment of our shrubs.

I know now that it was this 'landing chore' that wa most off putting of any of the work we had to tackle on our v We never minded the hours of digging, strimming, clea waterholes, mending fences, herding the stock, planting trees shrubs, mixing cement - you name it, we did it – for they wer in a day's work. If you can appreciate the difference.

One only has to attempt this ordeal of landing, clambe up the large slippery rocks, then the small dry ones 'till fin onto a shingle strewn passage of moving nightmares to appreci the title we have given it – the stairway to hell.

I am sure if we had only been twenty years younger would not have seemed such an ordeal. But then we were no QED.

Luckily I seem to be able to blank these necessary a obligatory episodes out of my mind. And just get on with the ta at hand. Shirley, however, found it her most harrowing tim even though I tried to take as much of the heavy baggage onto own shoulders.

No matter how one looks at it these chores just have to done – otherwise not a task on the island would have b completed.

Before anyone believes that the island farm is all w drudgery and no play let me please dispel this thought with alacrity.

Many happy and memorable times were spent literally the first full year of residency. Like the visits from fr – some for short hours, to those who camped out for weeken longer.

119

A PINCH OF SALTEE

Once our cattle crush cum sheep race was installed the flock would then be herded into that area with the same procedure maintained.

The fun and games, dry wit and sly wisecracks, that emanated from the sheep scene would have made the basis for a wonderful J.B. Keane short story. Not a curse was used!

This annual task, together with the exporting of our calves, although tough physical chores, became the jovial highlights of each summer. They also became easier as experience, drawn from previous exploits, clicked into gear each time.

Seventeen guests over a weekend was the largest number during the first five years.

This party included our closest veterinary and medical friends with their extended families. Most of them camped out but a few, who drew the long straws, made it inside, that is, inside our incomplete cottage.

We bird watched, fished, swam, had target practice with a repeating 12 bore and ate barbecued fish, rabbit and steak each evening. And drank a keg of beer and a 'vineyard of wine'!

Patrick Wall, head of the FSA[13] of Ireland, had been out to visit me in Kenya when I was on the Maasai Mara. Not only is he a vet, but a medical doctor too, and whilst serving a two year stint on a mission station in Tanzania, performed more surgical operations than most specialists see in a lifetime! He is also a madly keen equestrian who hunts all winter long with various packs of hounds from Roscommon to the Wards in north county Dublin and then finishes off the season by competing in weekly hunter trials.

He is also a keen fisherman and a great man with children. This inevitably lead him to be besieged each morning and evening by the assembly of youngsters. Both Patrick's would ferry them

---

[13] Food Safety Authority of Ireland

121

out to Sophia and off they'd go around the island with half a dozen lines trailing.

Sometimes just my son, Patrick, would take two of them out in the dinghy which they thought was much more daring and therefore more fun.

Lots of Pollock – some of two to three kilos – were caught, a few mackerel and a crab or two found in our lone lobster pot sunk some fifty metres from the mooring.

P. Wall would fillet the catch on a perfectly formed tabletop boulder set about halfway up our shoreline. His expertise was greatly admired by the band of smiling sunburnt faces of the children.

Once packed in herbs and butter and wrapped in tinfoil this lowly thought of fish, the humble Pollock, provided a mouth watering starter, or main course, at our evening 'braai' in the boma.

On one occasion while the two Patricks and most of the gang were 'gone fishin', I took the rest to watch birds on the southern cliffs. This is also the area where the sheep love to stay. Carvill brought his very young son, Ozzie, hopping, skipping and at times carrying him on his shoulders. He loved every minute of this new experience. When we arrived at a grassy knoll above a Disneyesque bay we call Smuggler's Cove, we (six or seven of us) sat down to watch the activity on the cliffs about one hundred metres away.

There were four or five young children with us whose respective fathers pointed out the different birds – gulls, fulmars, razorbills, kikkiwakes, terns.

Some of us moved away to find a colony of puffins a little to the west and north of the cliffs. After an hour or so we all met up on a path back to the homestead. Some children were being carried, others walked.

The fishing party had just returned and we all then met up in the boma deciding on what to cook and who was on fire duty – making the barbecue fire and getting everything prepared.

A PINCH OF SALTEE

Suddenly someone called for Ozzie. No one knew where he was – or more dramatically – could remember when last any one had seen him. After searching all areas around the homestead and beach, the brain cells got into overdrive and the two brothers-in-law Carvill and Dorman worked out who carried who, where and when. Something clicked.

Four of the party left in a hurry to retrace their footsteps up the island. The rest of us prepared the meal.

After about half an hour we saw the 'hunting party' returning over the skyline and yes - there was Ozzie riding his father's shoulders.

When they arrived finally at the boma we heard the full descriptive tale of the lost and found. During the bird watching session Ozzie was sitting on the grass beside the adults. Several of us moved off to view other species and some to the sheep and cattle.

Father thought brother-in-law had him – brother-in-law thought the reverse.

Meantime Ozzie was left on his own on the grassy knoll playing with the daisies and listening to the bird calls. Quite oblivious of the fact that everyone else had departed. Such happiness, such mirth. The ever embraceable arms of Bacchus enveloped us all throughout that joyous evening. Ozzie never knew anything about the anxiety felt amongst the entire party.

We all look back on that incident with even more trepidation than then. Now we demand regular head counts from all visitors during their island stay.

I had worried, from the very outset, about the possibility of losing stock over cliff edges – for whatever reason.

This did occur on a number of occasions, mostly for unaccountable reasons. Sometimes we were lucky and found the living culprit. Sometimes only the skeleton.

A PINCH OF SALTEE

The first of these involved three Galway ewes. It would have been about 11.30am on another lovely summer's day when we heard a boat hooting at us near the homestead. Fortunately all of us were working in the haggard.

I rushed down to the water's edge and listened to the lobsterman's shouts.

"Ye have some ewes down over the cliffs on the eastern side about halfway along. Near the waterhole. OK?"

I shouted back my acknowledgement and returned to get Shirley, Patrick and Liezel – some rope, a couple of jembes and a pick axe.

We started the search below *Cabots* on the eastern side and found the ewes below *Shirley's* some four hundred metres further south.

They were together and didn't seem too troubled by their misadventure. We were looking down from a good ten metre drop to vicious craggy rocks. All the cliffs in this area were inhabited by nesting Fulmars. They became exceedingly worried by our presence and put on an aerial display only Farnborough could rival.

Just to the south of *Shirley's* is a special Cormorant nesting mound – on an outcrop of land totally taken over by these gangling foragers of the ocean. At least sixty nests huddle together in a six square metre rock-strewn maternity wing.

It was possible to climb down the cliff face below them. This became our start off point of descent. All four of us ventured down, spearheaded by Patrick. I only went halfway and became the photographer. Almost every event had been catalogued pictorially by either myself or Shirley since the island challenge had begun.

Luckily the ewes were not too keen on breaking rank which made it easier for Patrick to catch them. He and Liezel pushed and pulled the first two up to where I was positioned. The sheep then realised they could climb the rest of the way on their own. Shirley was left down below holding onto the remaining ewe. Pat returned to assist her in guiding it up the cliff.

There had been adequate grazing along the shoreline and fresh water lay in pools kept full by the overflow from *Shirley's*. They could have survived for many days if not detected by the lobstermen. Their thick fleeces would have cushioned their crashing descent – if indeed that had been the case?

A repeat of this sheep rescue occurred a further three times, in different places, over the next four years.

A very different rescue – of our first born pedigree Kerry bull *Saltee Little Millennium Patrick* – took place on the west side of the island about five hundred metres south of the homestead.

This time we had Mickey, his son Jack, Bobby Stafford, and a couple of Jack's school chums out visiting us. They had brought a dozen new ewes to bolster our flock numbers.

Having herded them down to the southern slopes to join up with the resident flock we then inspected the Kerries who were grazing on the eastern side near *Patrick's*.

The herd was one short – *Millennium Patrick*. A very strange omission as he was not only a prominent horned creature but also the pretender to the throne.

First thoughts, fleeting across my mind, was that Uinseánn, our senior bull, and he had had a battle of strength and *MP* had lost. Although blessed with a fine pair of strong horns, reminiscent of a Spanish fighting bull, he was a year younger and therefore not carrying the weight of the 'leader of the pack'!

We fanned out, to cover every cove and cliff and hopefully discover a live but, perhaps, humiliated animal.

I returned to the homestead to make ready the veterinary kitbag, ropes, beef nuts and any implements that might be needed.

After about thirty minutes one of the youngsters, huffing and puffing like billyoh, emerged through the bracken at the back of the homestead.

A PINCH OF SALTEE

"We've found him. He's stuck like a statue down on the rocks near the fence. He's alive."

I immediately gave the lad a drink to cool and calm him down. He was joined by Jack who asked for a bucket of water and some rope to take back.

We found the group. And a very weak ribby looking bull. Behind him was a mire of manure. He had obviously been down there for quite some days. He would be very dehydrated.

The bucket of water, now only half full due to the bumpy ride it had received, was offered. He perked up at the first touch and taste.

We then used the bucket, as the carrot on a stick, held slightly in front to exhort him into movement. He did attempt a step or two, pushed from the rear by Mickey and Bobby.

Periodically he was given a drink. The bait was working. I clambered up the cliff with the bucket whilst the others pushed and pulled him along the rocks to an easier strip of grassland that ran down to the shore.

After a worrying forty-five minutes they managed to get him up onto the bracken. He then planted himself – not interested in another step in any direction.

I brought the water bucket to him and placed it under his head. Stupidly I too planted myself with the bucket. He bent down to drink – I leaned closer. CRACK like a rifle shot! Up came his head in a circling motion. His horns hit my right arm a lightening strike. I thought it was broken. The pain was brutal. I fell back into a thick bed of bracken. I saw stars for a moment or five. Then everything was vividly portrayed as in a flash from a camera. I was in a very very dangerous position. I remember witnessing a matador being gored and thrown by a rampant Spanish bull – just like this fellow.

I was up on my feet in that same flash, my arm numbed from the blow. I moved away. It was Mickey standing beside me, holding, questioning.

A PINCH OF SALTEE

The bull never moved. His eyes, however, focused directly on me. There was a fire within.

Never show fear I remembered being told on numerous occasions. My arm wasn't broken. Just numb and sore. I undid the rope around his horns and told Bobby to belt him on the rump.

He had finished the water, wasn't interested in the nuts and now sauntered off up the hill bellowing for all he was worth. He was obviously announcing his return to the herd in no uncertain manner.

No matter what breed of a bull one should never trust him. I had just been a touch too 'at ease' with Millennium Patrick that once. A warning I took onboard.

Another rescue act involved Patrick, myself, Bobbie and Jack. The latter two were going fishing, out beyond the islands, and had dropped in to see how we were faring. A neighbourly thing to do in rural or maritime Ireland.

Pat and I had counted the stock earlier on that day – we had been digging out Patrick's waterhole and the herd had come down for a drink. There was one bull calf missing. We then set out on a 'cliff hunt' and located the beast right down on the rocky shore below that very waterhole. He seemed in good condition and nothing, no limb, was broken. But, there was no way that just the two of us could ever get him back up onto terra firma. We were on the island by ourselves so I was prepared to contact Bobby and Mickey when, hey presto, we had two visitors – and able ones too.

I cut a 15 metre length of nylon rope and armed with feed, veterinary kit and implements we set out to retrieve one lost soul.

About one hundred metres north of where he was lay a rocky outcrop that allowed Bobby and Patrick to climb down without too much trouble armed with rope and bucket of feed.

Jack and I shadowed them from atop the cliffs edge. There was a sheer drop of twenty metres or so to the bull calf. How had he got there is a question unanswerable.

A PINCH OF SALTEE

"He's effing ok and he has a pool of effing clean fresh water too. Jes' look where he's been effing grazing will yer. He's right as effing rain down here."

All this was broadcast to the world by an effervescent Radio Bobby. Pat and he grabbed hold of the calf (approximately 200kgs) as Bobby fashioned a rope halter around his head with Pat holding the length of trailing rope.

Now the fun commenced. Little bull calf was quite happy where he was thank you, and, stubborn is as stubborn does, he refused to budge. The way ahead was a rocky and undulating one. And he just was not interested in cooperating.

Let me suffice to say that the serene, ozonic clarity of the atmosphere turned a deeper blue clouded screen of cynical sarcasm with impassioned haste. I wished for Mr. Webster to have been present. He could surely have added a page or two under the letters c,f and s!

It had been a stop start one hundred metres with falls up, falls down and falls over the rocky terrain. Despite the curses a lot of laughter also rose up from the depths.

When finally they arrived at the bottom of the shelf, up which we intended dragging the calf, I sent Jack down to catch hold of the rope and return with it to the surface. I, meantime, had found a suitable outcrop of rock around which the rope could be tightened.

Pat and Bobby shoved from below. Jack and I pulled from above. Eventually we got the bull to the surface, untied him and drove him up the hill to where the herd had gathered. They had heard our verses of comedy. He bellowed his head off and so did his mother in reply. We wondered if she would allow him back on the teat after such an absence. She certainly would love to rid herself of the built up pressure in her udder. We left them circling each other and hopefully getting to know and re-register each other's special odour.

By next morning everything was calm. She, the perfect suckler mother, had accepted him back.

A PINCH OF SALTEE

These were some of the happy endings. Unfortunately in a later chapter you will learn of the tragedies.

David Cabot, International Ornithologist

Ornithological Research on Little Saltee, Co. Wexford - By David Cabot.

Islands, especially uninhabited ones, have always fascinated naturalists as microcosms of wild nature where mammals, birds, insects and all forms of plant life can get on with their business unaffected and unsullied by the immediate impacts by man. For the scientist islands are also marvellous outdoor laboratories where the numbers and population dynamics of birds can be studied more easily than on the mainland where their distribution patterns become blurred and confusing. There is nothing more definitive than a small island such as Little Saltee where the boundaries are set and the plant and animal populations confined to a manageable area. For the ornithologist the major

A PINCH OF SALTEE

attraction of islands is breeding seabirds. Ireland is fortunate in possessing a complex coastline and hundreds of islands that are especially attractive to seabirds. Sixteen different kinds of seabirds, excluding the terns and the common and black-headed gull, nest on the islands of Ireland.

The Saltees are amongst the most important islands for breeding seabirds not only because of the diversity of species and total numbers nesting but also because the birds are so accessible and are easily observed, almost at arm's length. On Great Saltee twelve seabird species breed, some in exceptionally large numbers, while on the smaller Little Saltee – a sort of poor cousin of its much larger relation - only nine, sometimes ten, breed.

Why are the Saltees so important for seabirds? The surrounding waters are teaming with fish life, essential to support not only the adults but also the vast army of young birds reared every year who, with their parents, would add up to some 200,000 individuals that must be fed several times a day July. The islands also possess a wide range of cliff nesting habitats, catering for all the specialist requirements of the different species. The evolution of birds has ensured that birds don't compete for the same resources, food or nesting sites - the selection of breeding partners is a another story where fierce competition does occur, driven by different imperatives to ensure genetic health of the species – so each species occupies a particular cliff habitat. Puffins nest in holes, generally in steep sloping ground, along cliff tops while guillemots require flat rock surfaces on cliff faces. Cormorants require flat toped cliffs while kittiwakes need ledges on vertical cliffs.

As a schoolboy I was invited in 1956 to an ornithological conference in Oxford, organised by one of England's most brilliant ornithologists Dr. David Lack. There I met an equally intellectually brilliant John Barlee, an Irishman and graduate of Trinity College Dublin, who was lecturing in Oceanography at the Royal Naval College, Dartmouth. John had

A PINCH OF SALTEE

spent his undergraduate days in the 1940s roaming around Ireland and visiting islands. He was a dazzling photographer, an early pioneer of bird flight photography with the 35 mm "miniature" camera and published a book Birds on the Wing (Collins 1947) that contains many shots taken on the Saltee Islands. John had also spent some time with the late Major Ruttledge in establishing the Bird Observatory on Great Saltee Island. John was so enthusiastic about the Saltee Islands when we spoke at Oxford that they were on the top of the list of places to visit when I first came to Ireland in 1959. A few days on Great Saltee convinced me that the Saltees were one of the top ornithological sites in Ireland. Because Little Saltee was difficult to land on that island was always ignored and sort of overlooked by ornithologists. It was also smaller with less complex cliff structures and with fewer seabirds. In those days everyone went just to Great Saltee. But being somewhat intrepid and always curious to push into generally untrodden pastures one summer I managed to persuade Redmond Wheeler, a Dublin ornithologist with a penchant for miniature boat travel – regarded by some as a somewhat risky proposition - to ferry me across from Great to Little Saltee.

Since that first landing I have returned every year to Little Saltee to count, ring and retrap birds that we had ringed in earlier years, establishing an unbroken record of 43 years fieldwork. It is only through such long-term studies that one can develop an understanding about population dynamics including migrations, mortality, longevity and productivity. Our work is focused on two species – the cormorant and the fulmar petrel. We also follow closely census and ring shags and razorbills. Other seabirds are only censused each summer so that we can follow the general trends of their populations. Over the years the island fieldwork has been supported by numerous friends and colleagues but three stand out for their sustained assistance – Dr. Michael Greer-Walker during the early days; Professor Brian West during the middle period and currently Maurice Cassidy. So what have we been doing and how do we do it?

Because most of us are in full time occupations and lead rather full lives our expeditions to Little Saltee are often pressured, intense operations. Sometimes we are up at 5am in Dublin to drive down to Kilmore Quay

A PINCH OF SALTEE

usually on a Saturday morning towards the end of May where we inflate a small rubber dingy on the slip and then head for Little Saltee. The island can be quite a treacherous place for landing on and launching from, but over the years we have learnt where to land according to wind direction and speed and the status of the tide. Sometimes we have had to land under quite dodgy conditions like on the east coast rocks, accompanied by a drunken swell, scrambling ashore, then pulling the boat and heavy engine behind us. During the early days we had the luxury of being ferried across by the wonderful Willie Bates and John Power and, in a sense, that was simpler and cleaner because they would land us on the rocks in a punt and then go off, later plucking us off the rocky shoreline at the end of the day. So after a brief period of smoothing down our feathers and maybe a sandwich or two we start our work, which follows a standard procedure each year.

We start at Henry's farmstead, I walk along the cliff top with Maurice on the rocks below. Our objective as we work southwards is to catch as many of the incubating fulmars as we can. I have a strong 3 m bamboo pole with a net at the end and Maurice has a queer kind of net, very wide and broad attached to a bamboo pole. I gently pick up each incubating fulmar, record its ring number into a hand recorder or ring it if it's un-ringed. Some nests are too low on the cliff for me so Maurice deals with these but his great value is picking up the birds that I have failed to capture because I was not quick enough or missed because they were nervous and flew off the nest, down the cliff trying to get lift. He catches quite a few of the birds I miss. If any of his captures are ringed he shouts up the number and if not he rings the fulmar. Thus we slowly proceed around the island trying to capture every single nesting fulmar. As we move along I visually census the number of puffins and razorbills sitting on the water off their cliff nesting sites; shag nests are counted and clutch size noted and if there are young they are ringed. We also note the approximate number of breeding seagulls – great black-backed, lesser black-backed and herring gulls, without doing any detailed census. We also record the number of dead Manx shearwaters we find along the cliff tops.

Then we come to the first cormorant colony on the first headland along the south coast. Every nest is recorded with details of numbers of eggs or

132

young or eggs/young. All young cormorants old enough for ringing are then ringed. If the young ones are well developed, close to fledging, it is a hard task to round them up as they are quite mobile and make for the cliff tops, torn between jumping off or having better sense and staying behind. If the birds are well developed we try to turn them into the long grass or bracken where they are quite content to bury their heads in the vegetation, thinking they are evading us. As they lie there, ostrich-like, we pull back one of their legs to clip a metal ring onto it, and then leave the cormorant in its ignorant bliss. We then move out of the colony as fast a possible to minimise any disturbance that we may have caused.

Each metal ring we put on young cormorants, adult fulmars and any other seabird is individually numbered and with a return address c/o British Museum, London SW7. If one of our ringed cormorants is subsequently shot by a Frenchman, Spaniard or Portuguese, or found drowned in a fish net or found washed up on the shore the finder usually reports it to the British Museum and then the British Trust for Ornithology, who run the ringing scheme with financial support from the Irish Wildlife Service, informing us of the finding circumstances.

We continue to proceed around the island, ringing and censusing until we return to Henry's farmstead, often tired, seldom exhausted. The whole operation takes between 6-7 hours, non-stop, hard physical work. I have had two bad cliff falls, once tumbling down eastern cliffs after a foothold gave away in a boulder clay earth cliff. Fortunately I was fit and rolled down the cliff, head over heels several times like a commando over sharp rocks before arriving at the bottom where I lay still, extremely frightened to move any limb or neck in case a bone had been broken. After gingerly checking very slowly the movement of each limb it was a wonderful relief to discover that the only damage was a broken watchstrap. I mention this tale as a caution for anyone clambering over the cliffs – they are dangerous.

The final task – but we may sometimes do this as our first task on our visit, depending upon weather - is to census the occupied nest sites of the fulmars breeding on the cliff ledges and sometimes well concealed in cliff holes. This is best done from the boat gradually travelling around the island. This method provided a much more accurate census of fulmar

A PINCH OF SALTEE

nests many of which are unable to be seen either from the cliff top or from walking along the cliff base.

Sometimes we manage several day trips to the island to ensure that we have caught and ringed all the birds, especially if the breeding of the cormorants have not been synchronised and the young are at all different stages of life. Also fulmars need checking too as the males and females share the incubation of the single egg and one trip we may only catch one of the pair. We have also stayed overnight to catch roosting adult cormorants in the hope of controlling birds we have already ringed.

Returning to Kilmore Quay in the evening, tired and often elated by what we achieved during the day, we break the boat down on the pier and then treat ourselves to a wonderful seafood supper in Kilmore Quay.

The year 2003 was important for me. My dear friend John Barlee sadly died in 2002. His widow Laura asked me to spread John's ashes on the Saltee Islands and this I did at the end of our fieldwork, scattering them at the southern end of the island, over the grass where puffins tread and Manx shearwaters haul their bodies down into their subterranean nesting burrows. It was a sad journey for me but for John, who loved the islands so much, it was the perfect resting place.

Population dynamics of the fulmar, *Fulmaris glacialis*, breeding on Little Saltee, Co. Wexford.

The study commenced in 1960 when fulmars were noted prospecting the island. The first breeding occurred in 1962 (5prs) and since then the population has increased to 187 prs (2003) with earlier peaks of 306prs in 1995 and 276 in 2001. Intensive ringing of adults and pulli commenced in 1974. Totals of 790 adults and 640 pulli have been ringed to 2003 inclusive. A total of 1,557 adults, mostly incubating birds, have been re-trapped of which 56 per cent had previously been ringed on the island apart from the following birds: an adult ringed Fair Isle (1984); single pulli ringed at Gairsay, Orkney (1972), Puffin Island, Co. Kerry (1972 –

134

two pulli), Yell Sound, Shetland (1981), North Rona (1984) and Bardsey (1986). Despite large numbers having been ringed on nearby Great Saltee by Oscar Merne and his seabird study group, only one ringed adult had been recaptured on Little Saltee. This record, together with one Little Saltee bird recaptured on Great Saltee, demonstrates remarkable site fidelity. Little Saltee ringed birds have been recovered in Cork (1); Wales (1), Cumbria (1), Lancashire (1), Scilly Islands (2), Finistere (3), Norfolk (1), Netherlands (1) and Sweden (1). Annual productivity (well grown chick per breeding pair) was a mean 0.51 (range 0.34 - 0.82) ± 0.13 sd for the period 1976-1986, compared with 0.16 - 0.52 recorded from the long term study at Eynhallow, Orkney, Scotland. Based on an estimated annual adult mortality rate of 88-92% (calculated from the Eynhallow study) and the mean productivity rate from Saltee 27 young will survive from 100 pairs to be recruited into the breeding population each year. A database, containing some 3,000 records of birds ringed, re-trapped, controlled and recovered, has been established.

Publications:
Cabot, D. 1999. *The Natural History of Ireland*. HarperCollins, London. pp. 373-4.

b) Population dynamics of the cormorant, *Phalacorcorax carbo*, breeding on the Little Saltee, Co. Wexford.

The study commenced in 1960 when the first detailed annual census of the breeding population (number of breeding pairs, and clutch size - based on eggs/chicks per nest) was carried out. Since then all available pulli, totalling 10,174 from 1960 to 2002 inclusive, have been ringed. Investigations into the diet (regurgitated food brought to the colony during the breeding season) have been completed. Pesticide levels in eggs have been monitored over several years. During the 43 year study period so far the mean size of the breeding colony was 300 ± 50 sd pairs showing a significant increase in numbers recorded from 1987 onwards, a delayed response to the cormorant's protected status under the Wildlife Act, 1976. An analysis of 9,006 pulli ringed showed there have been 1,167 recoveries or 13.3% of those ringed, to 1st April 1997. Most - 38.8% - were shot; 36.8% found dead; 16.7% trapped or caught in nets; 3.7% unknown causes; 2.4% sick-injured; 0.6% oiled and 1.5% miscellaneous. Birds during their first year of life suffered two to three times higher reported mortality than older birds from being shot or tapped in nets. Little Saltee cormorants exhibit more positive migratory movements than birds from other colonies. Reported recoveries of all aged birds from France have been 21.6%; Spain (7.7%) and Portugal (2.1%). It is intended to continue the project until at least 2010, making it one of the longest and continuous studies of the species in Western Europe.

Publications:

West, B., Cabot, D. and Greer-Walker, M. (1975). The food of the cormorant *Phalacrocorax carbo* at some breeding colonies in Ireland. *Proc. R. Ir. Acad.* **75** B: 285-304.

Cabot, D. 1999. *The Natural History of Ireland.* HarperCollins, London. pp. 367-72

Maurice Cassidy – able assistant to David Cabot

Chapter Eight

Tractor and Implements – Cottage – Spiral Staircase – The Rescue

Having Mickey Strong onboard was undoubtedly a turning point in our endeavours. Some challenges didn't now seem to be insurmountable. We had an ally with an extended family of friends. A most precious ingredient in any project.

He knew I was looking for an old grey Ferguson tractor with a couple of implements. I needed to be able to cut bracken, in certain areas, at an early age. I also wished to till a couple of hectares a year and hopefully plant up new grass leys.

Early in 2002 he phoned to say he had 'a right good Fergie' which I could buy. He recommended I offer a certain figure, be prepared to pay another couple of hundred to have it rewired and get a new battery. He would tinker with it and have it up and working by June. Newly painted 'it would be magnificent' he added. I said "go ahead, do the necessary. I would put my cheque in the post."

"No need to do that, I'll settle it and sure next time you're down you can fix me up. It will be just right for you."

By the time we next got down to Kilmore Quay and visited him he had found a hay cutter and a disc harrow that would also be right for the island. The cutter bar, the old scissors style, was up in the mountains on Paddy Lacey's smallholding. It was a good twenty minutes drive, "lovely views up there" but he couldn't come with us just then as he had someone about to buy one of his tractors.

Shirley, Oscar and I set off with directions from him. It certainly was a lovely high rolling part of the country with, sure enough, the most spectacular panoramic vista of Carnsore Point to Hook Head from a well forested mountain top.

138

A PINCH OF SALTEE

We missed the correct turnoff on the first sortie but thanks to our cell phone managed to find the farm without further trouble.

Paddy wasn't there "but wouldn't be long now" said his wife Ann. "Have a look around anyway. There might be other things of interest to you."

Shirley and Oscar went off for a walk through the forest whilst I rooted around a scrap yard of curiosities.I espied the cutter bar and gave it the once over. Although an ancient model, in comparison to 2000 editions, it looked almost new. I hoped it had a spare blade. There were tractors, mowers, front loaders, electric saws, steel baths, tanks – you name it, Paddy had it.

Next to this display was an enchanting donkey foal on a long rope tied to a pole. He had plenty of grass to graze and a tub of water was within his reach. When Shirley and Oscar returned we made quite a hit with the foal who within minutes became almost over friendly. They are such gentle creatures and immense value on small holdings as beasts of burden – even to this day.

Paddy returned and showed me the hay cutter which did have a spare blade so a deal was struck. He also said he had a nice quaint wood burner (stove) going cheaply which he showed me. Mickey had mentioned to him I was looking for a pot belly stove but this would be a good substitute he said. We also agreed a price so it had been a most constructive drive up in the country.

On returning to Mickey I congratulated him on finding me those two important items. The stove would be ideal for the cottage – downstairs in the dining room. We could cuddle around it on wet days and it would eradicate the damp of winter when lit up each spring. Both items for €250 – not a bad deal I reckoned. I had also seen some grand sized tree trunks lying around the place at Paddy's. I needed three rounds approximately six inches in depth. Could he please ask Paddy for me?

I could see he was bursting to tell us something so I assisted by saying, "go on say it or show it." He beckoned us to follow him behind his house to the workshop.

A PINCH OF SALTEE

"That's yours so it is," as he proudly patted the bonnet of an ancient decrepit looking Ferguson tractor.

"Does it work?" I asked with, most probably, a large frown on my forehead.

"Oh, be dad it does and rightly too." I stalked it, then walked all around it, then jumped into the cold steel seat and let out a roar, "Ye haa" – just what I wanted. "Well done old scout. It'll be brilliant." I was like a child again – on my first tractor at Rath House the original home of my cousins the Blands. JB taught me how to drive a tractor and later on my first car there. That was way back in the forties. Wow, what a long time ago that seemed.

Shirley thought I was mad – once again! How on earth would we get it out, think of all the hassle, where would we land it and what if it wouldn't start? You know, all the sensible thoughts of a logical loving partner who only really wanted a quiet easy life in retirement.

I gave her a big hug and kiss, took Mickey's hand in gratitude and said "how about a hot cuppa to celebrate."

We trundled into his kitchen where Jemma and the kids were already having a snack. We sat down beside their pot belly stove which was giving out a lovely warmth to the room. Mickey opened with "you won't recognise it when I've finished all the little things and given her a coat or two of paint. She'll be as good as new then. Able to do all the things you want on the island."

Over a lovely hot mug of tea we discussed the weight and how difficult it would be to get it loaded onto the raft and then off again out on the island.

"Sure it'll be half the weight of the last load you took out, even with the mower attached."

"That's fine then. I can see there should be no difficulty in getting it loaded. We'll dock the raft on the slipway – let the tide go out – and then build a ramp of planks up the raft. You can be the driver Mickey – that picture will make the front page of the Echo," I added with a voluminous chortle. Shirley kept saying 'we were mad – the lot of you'. The kids were all agog at the idea and all wanted to ride the raft on the way out.

"What if it sinks? Can you swim girls? We wont worry about the boys – they'll look after themselves – won't you lads?" The girls were really up for it, the lads a triffle circumspect I felt. Sure wasn't it always that way too when we were growing up?

He enquired if we were in a hurry or could he show us a disc harrow he had found? "Its only down the road, in fact quite close to the Quay." Shirley and I decided to go and see it, as at that very moment, some visitors arrived and I somehow knew there was business to be done on Mickey's side. It never ended at that household.

He gave us directions and off we went. The harrow was out the back of Robert Moore's house. It looked in good condition but a might rusted. It probably hadn't been used for sometime. The discs, however, were sharp and not dented. 'A good oil and grease with a couple of rounds of a field would see it right' I murmured to myself. And the price was right. Unfortunately no one was home so we left without concluding the deal.

Next day Mickey showed me a portable cement mixer which he offered at a reasonable price. It wasn't too cumbersome or heavy so it would be transportable in *the banana boat*. He would tinker with it and have it ready for use in no time at all. I loved his optimism.

This trip proved to be a great buying spree. Finally and probably the most important item, was an 110 kw generator. Old but small and light, Mickey had bought it at a car boot sale and it was mine for €150. I agreed. Once again I needed his guarantee 'to be delivered in full working order'. He confirmed it would – no problem.

With that on the island we had loads of possibilities to look forward to. Electricity in all the houses and outside if need be. No more scissor shearing of the sheep. Now we could have electric clippers. All tools, drills, the like and now the cement mixer could be worked off our new 'genny'. Things were looking up. All we had to do was get them out there.

Once the new roof had proved its worth I set about designing the interior of the cottage.

The Perspex panels seemed to keep the internal temperature at 65 degrees in the non sunny months – so I was well pleased with that innovation. In the summer temperatures reached the 80's so I was happy to have the two doors opposite each other – south/north facing. When open they allowed a temperate onshore breeze to circulate.

Patrick, Liezel and I had attended the annual Bannow Rathangan Agricultural Show the year before. It takes place on the farm of Eddie White, a few miles out of Kilmore Quay on the Duncormick Road. It is an enormous one-day show and we found it beautifully organised and full of interesting exhibits.

One of these was a display by Finbar Buttimer of metal and wrought iron work. Included in his repertoire was an elegantly simple spiral staircase. I spoke with him for quite a while about my idea of having one such item for the cottage.

"Just give me the measurements, and idea of the design you would like. I'll make it and fit it for you." Straight to the point we got – an approximate price was agreed. I said I would phone him through the measurements and I would want it ready the following spring.

"No problem – I'd be proud to do something really nice for such a historic place. See you then," was his parting remark as he left to satisfy some other customers.

Upstairs in the loft would be our master bedroom. I needed a wardrobe, dressing table, wash stand, two bedside tables and of course a comfortable mattress on a pine bedstead. As much of this would have to be easily portable, light and unbreakable. I chose pine as it is easy to mix and match.

A PINCH OF SALTEE

The pine floor Patrick and I had installed the previous year, and very luckily coated with two dressings of a top varnish, had matured like good wine.

I found various items at Buckley's Auction Rooms during the winter. My niece Valerie Kiernan gave us the dressing table, our South African neighbours contributed some carpets with another couple of neighbours, Derrick and Patricia Hill giving us a liquor trolley. Shirley had decided to replace the mattress of our spare bedroom with a new one so we brought the old one down to the island. I bought the pine bed in Stillorgan – all packed into two easily carried cardboard containers. The wardrobe I found in Atlantic Hardware. A pre-packed DIY unit of canvass covering hanging area and shelves. It zips up to shut out insects, etc.

We brought out these items in the spring prior to the staircase. We had a ladder up to the loft which was approximately 3 metres above the cobbled floor.

Our first nights spent in the cottage were very special – especially so as we had idyllic weather.

We are both early risers – me to make the first cups of tea and to let Oscar out for his pee run. Shirley to tune into weather forecasts and the news!

That first awakening was something quite remarkable. We were almost imploded deeper into the bed, if that was possible. The apex of the roof was only 2½ metres above us and something hit it with a deafening thud. Then lots of scratching and scraping noises while we guessed the culprit.

One of our Lesser Black Back gulls - sentinels of the homestead - had landed! After a couple of minutes it hailed all others in the neighbourhood. That early morning crescendo lasted a good five minutes. No need to have an alarm clock – that's for sure!

Never, since first we set up residency, have these gulls been afraid of or been intimidated by us. Instead of only having a ruin gable end as their sentry post they now had an 8½ metre roof top ridge available for their friends to visit with them. The concrete barges running up these gables were proving to be ideal landing strips. They were becoming well toileted too!

I would return with steaming tea and we would then listen to RTE radio 1 'till 8.00am. During this hour it was fascinating to watch the first light of dawn. The eastern sun rising over the hill above the homestead, its rays penetrating through the see-through panels and gracing the southern wall inside the cottage, right beside out heads.

One of the first instruments to be placed on the end beam of the loft was a thermometer and beside it a barometer given to us by Patrick and Liezel. Essential pieces of furniture as we were to find out and rely on in the years that followed.

With our bedroom virtually completed it was now time to visualise the sitting room. We both agreed on cane furniture. The conservatory suite in Dublin was now 'past its sell by date' so I offered to buy a new suite for there and take the old one down to the island. I then bought a single pine bed and mattress which would double as a chaise longue and overflow sleeping quarters.

At Buckley's I found four cottage style chairs with raffia seats and the wood painted red. " Ideal" I said to myself and especially at the mark down price of €20. These would be ideal around the folding pine table Tony and Etain had given us. It was their first piece of furniture when they got married. Nice to have a piece of Shirley's family history in the cottage.

We prayed for high pressure and got rewarded. Two trips in Sophia brought all these plus a variety of plants out on a serene day. Both times we managed to bring Sophia right onto the kelp area between the rocks which made off loading so much easier. With only the two of us someone very definitely was looking down and affording us his assistance. By landing in such a way it meant no off loading from boat to dinghy and back again. Quite a relief! And it was a warm sunny day so we were both in shorts and shirts and enjoying the task of off loading and carrying just this once.

A PINCH OF SALTEE

I had bought terracotta tiles during the winter for the other half of the cottage's floor and had them stored at Mickey's. Shirley and I would have to lug up barrow loads of sand from the one solitary stretch of beach when it wasn't under kelp or rotting seaweed. This was a chore we hated. And I really wasn't meant to be doing that sort of thing anyhow. Nor was Shirley.

During May I ordered timber for a new roof I wished to put on part of the old homestead building. I wanted to store hay for the stock and feed it to them from January onwards. Whilst discussing the timber order with Bobby I half hinted at getting some ton and groove flooring. Perhaps he could find some second-hand for me? As quick as a diving porpoise he came at me "how much you want. I can get as much as you feckin need. Genuine. I'll make it a good effing price too".

"I'd need 4 metres square".

"No effing problem. And do you know where it's going to be from? The Wooden House no less. How about that for effing good luck."

"Wow, that's a bit of a touch" I responded. "It will tie in with a bit of local history too. Good thinking Bobby".

"Oh, its lovely timber, effing beautiful in fact. I've got the contract to rip it up and sell it on. So there – I'll see to it".

My idea now was to timber-floor the other half of the downstairs. Much easier on us. I could do the whole job myself. The tiles now would be used to floor the kitchen and bathroom. I would get Patrick or Robert to carry up the sand the following year. Mickey would do the tiling.

I had sufficient lengths of 4 x 2 timbers already on the island so next day I made the 'boxing' of the floor my task. This wasn't difficult and only took a couple of hours.

The sitting room would be 6" higher as we had boxed that in with larger timbers beneath its flooring. This made for a varied perspective within a confined space. Two very different rooms 'open plan' on one floor.

A PINCH OF SALTEE

The call from Finbar came to say that the staircase was ready. I asked him to please paint it and the railings a certain red, which I gave the number of, and if all was ok weather wise would arrange for its transportation out the following week.

Bobby was requested to please be available to pick it all up with his lorry and bring it to the slipway. Also to have the load of flooring timber ready to come out at the same time. Mickey was also asked to please assist. With Dave and his friend Eamonn we would have sufficient manpower to handle the entire cargo in *the banana boat.*

The spiral was almost three metre high by one and three-quarters of a metre wide and had a dozen steps. We covered the entire staircase in a giant pvc sack which builders use for transporting a ton of sand. This was to protect it from scraping any of the paintwork. It could well have been a missile of sorts it looked so mysterious. Also I didn't wish the prying eyes to see what was going on!

We loaded it up over the bow area of *the banana boat* with the two sets of railings alongside. The flooring took up the remainder of the space.

Bobby in his Cobra RIB accompanied Finbar and us in *Sophia.* We off loaded without problems and carried this amazing looking package up to the stable door of the cottage. The merry band of helpers also offloaded the flooring and carried it up to the high water mark. Shirley and I would do the rest in our own time.

My stable door to the cottage was one metre wide and the spiral staircase was one and three-quarters metres wide. An enigma! It just looked impossible an undertaking. Finbar said he could unbolt certain sections and get it through the doorway for reassembly within.

I held back with my bit of wisdom until all the 'f's' from Bobby had expired.

"Anyone here every opened a bottle of wine or are you all beer drinkers?" I questioned a perplexed group.

"Catch hold over there Mickey. Bobby you take that end. Finbar you go inside to receive it. Dave and Eamonn grab here please, whilst I direct you gentlemen."

"Oh yer effin good at that alright. So lets see how brainy you are. Right lads – lift," shouted Bobby and they all lifted.

As they approached the door I directed the two at the bottom of the object to move it sideways so that the two at the top end could corkscrew it through the opening.

Once the top end was inside, the rest was simple. A matter of twisting on its axis and operating it as a giant corkscrew.

"Effing marvellous," commented Bobby. "Who would have believed it?"

"I'm not the bright one," I admitted. "I phoned an engineering friend who told me how to work it. You can get twice the width of the opening through with this principle. Smart eh?" and we all laughed.

"Effing brilliant," commented Bobby once again.

Next we stood it upright. I had measured it for placement exactly halfway across the loft floor. Was I going to be right? Finbar had brought out a full range of tools just in case. But no – he had no need – it fitted. And there would be no cementing it into the ground either. The eight bolts on the platform joining the loft to the stairs would hold it rigid. The new wooden flooring, once positioned, would further encase its base.

Finbar had the whole fitting, including railings, finished within two hours. A masterful piece of craftsmanship. The others went off fishing and promised to drop some of the catch off on their way home. We returned Finbar and his tools, the likes which I longed to have on the island, to Kilmore Quay late in the afternoon. He had walked around the farm noting the rabbit population. I sensed he would like a return trip with his point 22. An immediate invitation went out to him.

We ate an early fresh fish supper at the Upper Deck that evening. Deirdre gave us a porthole window table so that we could look across to our island cottage whose roof reflected the amber warmth of the setting sun.

When the sea was this calm we felt that we were literally driving three miles down the road to a favourite restaurant. One very salient factor here, however, was that there would be no breathalyser testing on our return trip!

Tony and Etain had given us, as a Christmas present the previous year, the largest candle we had ever seen. I had a special place welded onto the outside of the spiral staircase for it. That evening we placed it in position and lit its three wicks. Perfection! Its warm glow cannoned around the walls onto the roof subsequently taking over the mantle from the last rays of sunshine telescoping through the downstairs porthole.

Over the next few days we carried up the pieces of flooring. I sorted out lengths of the well bronzed, burn marked pine strips, which certainly could tell a tale or three, if only?

Shirley cut them into sizes for me to nail down. Once she had finished that job she joined me in the final few squared metres of nailing and fitting. After a couple of hours we had our dining room. We moved the red table and chairs from the sitting area, the wine trolley to one of the walls, and potbelly stove donated by Dave was suitably placed in the western corner. This generous gift now meant we had two stoves so both cottages were now catered for.

With colourful 'throws' brought back from our trip to Mexico, wall hangings given as presents, some from India and South Africa, Indian rugs (bought in Camden Street!) and a library of books and magazines the look and feel of the place was almost as I had envisaged a few years previously. We were both well satisfied with our efforts.

At this juncture it meant we now had a cottage to live in and a spare bedroom for family or visitors.

A PINCH OF SALTEE

Our toilet facilities were even becoming more urbanised. We now had a 'portaloo' for those so inclined or the original P.K[14]. (picaninikia) out back of the haggard.

Our original bath, brought out in 1998. still resplendent outside the kitchen and overflowing with clear rainwater was where all washing up – of anything – took place. Kettles were boiled for hot water. It was always aplenty when needed.

I constructed a boardwalk from the kitchen door out and alongside the bath as the cobbles in that area were rather irregular and therefore uneven to stand on.

We had built up, in the dry stone method, around the bath placing a table top of Formica on one end for the drying up area. Everyone took this chore in turns when visitors were with us. Otherwise Shirley usually washed and I dried.

Three dining places provided us with variety. Breakfast and lunch could be taken on the picnic table in the haggard, afternoon tea and evening/sun downer/drinks at the bay table and supper in the boma. Come mid to late September it was warmer to have supper by candle light inside the cottage. The occasional breakfast, if overcast, blustery or raining was also now taken inside.

As Bobby Stafford said on many an occasion "sure ye have the best of both effing worlds. And ye did it yourselves, feckin sure."

Weather plays such an enormous part in everything pertaining to the island. It, perhaps, wouldn't be such an issue if we lived out there permanently as in olden times. But with all the setting up and restoration work in progress, during the first five years, an alert watch had to be kept at all times.

One afternoon whilst Mickey and his team were working on the cottage roof I noticed that an off shore breeze was picking

---

[14] An outside toilet, usually at the end of the garden.

up. It had been calm and sunny since early morning. I was actually getting afternoon tea ready for the lads so a quick round table conference was called.

There was definitely a 'surge' building up with a westerly wind forcing increasingly high waves onto our shoreline.

Mickey was the most experienced sailor in our midst. He had seven years of shrimping and scalloping behind him. We had a close and long look at the scene. He agreed they should 'up tools' and set sail. It was 3.45pm – the sun was still high in the sky. It was a radiant Mediterranean blue.

The team moved down to get the dinghy ready for launching. As it had been such a calm day we had brought Sophia onto the kelp bed in the morning and left her there.

I have such a lot of fiddling little things to do in and around the homestead prior to leaving that it takes a good eight to ten minutes to tend to them all. Like shutting off the gas, closing all the doors, returning all tools and utensils inside, packing any rubbish into bags, collecting up ones private items – camera, radio, overnight bag and keys, etc., etc. Finally, checking that the gates and fence around the haggard are all secured. Then, and only then, can I proceed to the shore. This day I was without Shirley.

The lads meantime had launched the boats but I could see, as I trotted down the incline, that the surge was playing havoc with their attempts to keep the boats facing into the waves. This is absolutely essential for if they get turned by the wave's force and the sterns should get caught by this motion, their outboard engines could be submerged – even for seconds and that could prove dire.

When I arrived at the water's edge, the dinghy, with the two hired lads aboard, was about ten metres out into the surge. They were using paddles to keep themselves afloat and 'into the wind'. I jumped into *Sophia* who was being rocked about like a bucking bronco. Waves and spray were now excessive.

I attempted to get the engine started as Mickey and Jason pulled at the oars. It was a 'no go' situation with the engine, no matter what I did. Water had obviously penetrated the plugs.

A PINCH OF SALTEE

Their rowing had now got *Sophia* beyond the rampant surge but, although in calmer waters, this was the area of fast currents.

All we had to do was reach our mooring. It was less than seventy metres away. The dinghy was now alongside and we attached her painter to *Sophia*. They hadn't been able to start her engine either so all we had was manpower. The two youngsters came aboard *Sophia*.

Meantime I was attempting to radio Declan whom I had seen cruising out to the big island, on pickup duty, some thirty minutes earlier. He could come by on his return and collect us from the mooring.

With my head tucked down into my anorak to save myself and radio from wind, spray and banter I tried to make contact with anyone on channels, 6,8, 10, etc. but without any response. I came up for air after what seemed a short time and was astounded to see that we had been taken at least two hundred metres north of the mooring and indeed were speedily heading straight for *the Bridge*. I couldn't believe it. Everyone else was taking a pull at the oars but no headway was being made towards the mooring. We were being swept along by a very strong current.

I kept on calling Declan, the Harbour Master's office, and/or any other boat who could hear my plea – it was also a mayday SOS plea at this juncture.

Finally I was answered by the Rosslare Lifeboat services who asked all sorts of questions about my position, name of boat, size and how many onboard.

I didn't want their lifeboat – that would be ridiculous – as Kilmore Quay's very own, the Mary Margaret, was only a few miles away. But I didn't need them either to be called out. All I wanted was for someone to pass on the message to Declan, who wasn't answering my call, to pick us up. Rosslare was very persistent, keeping me on the blower and monitoring our position. It looked as if no one else could hear or cared about our plight. It was a worrying time for the Life Boat personnel as their aim is to save lives. Ours, to them, could well be a danger situation. An aura of frustration had crept into my crew.

We had now been carried over *the Bridge* and were drifting, away from the current into the middle of Ballyhealy Bay.

Some how, I wasn't at all worried, although I did sense a slight edge of anguish amongst the youngsters, two lads from Bridgetown we had hired for the day to assist Mickey with the roof. There wasn't anything wrong with *Sophia* or the dinghy. No leaks were showing. And the sea was quite calm. Neither engine would start!

I was kept occupied on the radio and hadn't seen the two flares go up over Kilmore Quay which meant that the Mary Margaret had been alerted. One of the lads drew my attention to this.

Declan was not responding to any of my or anyone else's calls. I, however, kept on trying to raise him. This nil response was maddening.

From sounding the alert to launching the Mary Margaret would be eight minutes – then add another six or so for them to get to us and we would be rescued by the RNLI.

We were now just sitting in *Sophia* and awaiting them. It was 4.50pm. We had been afloat and adrift for over forty minutes. The sun was still warm and the sky blue.

There was a flight of gannets bombarding a certain section of *the Bridge*. A shoal of whitebait was probably in view.

As I looked at the island from a completely new perspective – we had never ventured this far out into this bay before – it was interesting to note the comparison between the cliffs on its eastern side and the lowland pastures on the west. There was much more activity from fulmar, herring gull and tern on this side. A lot of cormorants were fanning their wings at the island's most northerly point. Then, as in a scene from the African Queen, I caught a glimpse of Declan's Tapaidh coming into view from around the western side. They looked a long way away.

A PINCH OF SALTEE

I pointed this out to Mickey and the crew who now suddenly looked overly pleased.

Almost at that same moment, one of the youngsters, Paul I think it was, shouted to say he could see the lifeboat leaving the harbour.

The race was on. Who would get to us first? A bit absurd I thought of who ever called the lifeboat.

Rosslare quickly put me right. It was them – their duty was to send the nearest lifeboat to the rescue. They were, rightly, doing their job.

But here they were coming out for nothing as Declan was on his way – as I had predicted thirty minutes previously. If only he had answered my calls!

Suddenly he responded on my radio – he could see us and would be alongside in three minutes. He hoped we were all ok. I replied that we were but questioned why he hadn't responded earlier. His radio went silent?

Both launches were rapidly approaching, the Mary Margaret from the north and Tapaidh from the west.

It was almost a dead heat – but Declan and Tapaidh made it! We threw them a line and they took us in tow. The two youngsters hurriedly jumped aboard Tapaidh as she closed beside us. They obviously wanted a safer footing!

I waved and shouted my thanks to the crew of the Mary Margaret under the coxswain ship of Brian Kehoe. He didn't look a happy man. I empathised with him, never wishing him or his expert band of volunteers to be dragged into this ridiculous situation.

However, safety is as safety does and we were all extremely grateful for their assistance and assuredness.

That night in Kehoe's the entire crew were treated to a belly full and some. I never did find out whether Declan knew, all along, about our 'little problem' and just showed up at the right moment. One of the unanswered riddles of the sea around the Saltees.

A PINCH OF SALTEE

When I phoned Shirley from Mill Road later that evening she nearly took the head off me.

"Why in heaven's name hadn't I dropped anchor when I saw we were being taken by the current?"

I couldn't answer. I was dumfounded by such a simple solution. Shirley, as I think I have said before, is the sailor in the outfit. I certainly hadn't been thinking like one – and neither had Mickey or any of them, for that matter. Perhaps they had been a trifle more terrified than I had originally thought. Foolish me.

I learnt a salutary lesson that day – one I shan't forget in a lifetime.

RNLI Mary Margaret at Kilmore Quay

Delight and Disaster

Anxious Moments. The craft's precious load.

Shirley and I are confident of its capabilities.

Majestic Sight

Knockane Uinseann **arrives safely**

**Stock
crush being
set in place**

**Trimming
feet**

Shirley at work
on her REPS
wall.

It's not all hard Work

Dave preparing *the banana boat*

Fully laden with Winter feed

The "Boma" prior to modernisation. The Nicholsons ;
Tony, Alex and Matthew with Patrick
and Liezel.

My daughter Dee Dee with Claire and Dougie at our "baytable"

Hardy KQ men bringing home the baby beef!

Soay sheep prior to release. Oscar in attendance.

Spiral staircase arrives at the homestead.

Part of the ground floor of Soay Cottage.

View, through the deer pen, of stock shed (right) and haggard.

The Boma" (foreground) and finished rooves. Achievement !

A PINCH OF SALTEE

Chapter Nine

Launching and Driving – Sophia Escapes –– Grandchildren – Calves Off - Farewell Sophia - Winters of Discontent

Early in March 2002 Patrick and I managed to take a week off and spend it together in Kilmore Quay. We had a number of projects to complete. I find it imperative to do the thing oneself or it doesn't get done. Cynical perhaps but honest and in reality factual.

One of these was to repaint *the banana boat* and get her launched. Without it my entire summer's project would crumble. However, to get Dave to actually do something outside his timber business, in or out of business hours, such as to 'make ready' his boat is not an easy task. Patrick is just too nice to push him but I certainly am not!

It does take quite a lot of organisation – but many hands make light work has always been a maxim of mine. So I pigeonholed Dave and the three of us got cracking on painting, welding extra cleats, and generally smartening her up.

Dave has a remarkable contraption tucked in at the back of his farmhouse. Its an ancient forklift – an enormous old machine with chains and gantry that lift the fork. Away it started after a couple of heaves and curses and within twenty minutes, and by some astute and quite outstanding driving and manoeuvring, Dave had *the banana boat* lifted onto its long trailer, already attached to his old banger.

With much glee we downed cups of coffee and cake produced at just the right moment by the good humoured Jacqui, Dave's partner. This was a fine morning – one of the few so far. Jacqui wanted to know why she and the children were not in her native Australia.

"We get real weather there" she kept reiterating. Both Patrick and I knew exactly what she was on about.

A PINCH OF SALTEE

the banana boat was launched an hour later and berthed just below the Guillemot lightship museum on the western pier. This was an ideal position for any of us to take her around to the slipway for loading.

Patrick and I attached our 15 hp outboard on and gave her a fifteen minute spin out and around the bay. All seemed well. That was now one major victory – metal boat in the water and ready to rock and roll. Full marks to Dave.

Our next project was the tractor. We drove over to Mickey, picked him up and set out for Dave Radford's farm up in the mountains overlooking the entire region. What magnificent views from up there. Dave was an engineer, an expert in rewiring engines. That's why he had our old vintage masterpiece.

Patrick was to drive the Fergie back to Mickey's. He had only driven a tractor in Underberg, on his sister's farm, for a few minutes, and that was some years ago.

We outlined the route he must take, all along good secondary roads with only a couple of crossings. He didn't seem perturbed.

Dave's farm and yard was up a winding narrow lane on a very steep incline. Mickey instructed Patrick how to drive, manage the clutch, brake, gears and throttle. After a few hiccups Patrick showed apprehension and was obviously worried by the steep descent to the road. Dave's son, miraculously appeared from nowhere, and offered to take it down with Patrick, standing up behind him, to see the various moves to make.

We gave them a five minute start and then followed. When we encountered them on the tar road Micky turned around and brought Dave's son back up to the farm whilst I gave Patrick a confidence boost and set him on his way. I watched as he clung closely to the left side of the road, every now and then swinging slightly out and then back into the curb as he tried to master the steering.

Mickey picked me up and we followed on down the road, now quite busy with late afternoon traffic.

A PINCH OF SALTEE

All of a sudden I cried out "oh my god! What is he doing?" as I saw Patrick performing a juggling act with his right hand and something, whilst his left couldn't quite control the steering wheel. He turned out onto the middle of the road, saw the oncoming traffic and turned hurriedly back to the inside, running up and along the bank. He had the sense to take it out of gear and apply the brakes.

Running from the car we now saw what had happened.

The exhaust pipe had jumped free and Patrick had instinctively caught it, lost driving concentration and had slightly panicked. So would I or probably anybody else too. Never mind, a burnt hand!

He wasn't too shaken, however, and after replacing the loosened pipe we set him on his way again. Patrick complained that 'my boots are too big and therefore I can't control the brake and clutch very well.'

"Take your time and just keep into your left. You'll be alright." And we departed. Mickey was now late for picking up his wife Jemma from where she worked. We went like the Billy goat, collected her, and then agreed to return to Baldwinstown village where there was a crossroads which Patrick would have to negotiate. And it had a pub!

It was a lovely evening and the three of us sat outside with our pints and Jemma's Vodka and White. I had one pint ready for Patrick on the table. We awaited his arrival.

I was more than a little 'agitatum'. I heard the tractor first and ran up the road to greet them waving Patrick to the opposite side to a space alongside Johnny Howlin's homestead wall.

Patrick looked completely shook – his eyes were streaming and his face was a puffy pink.

"What's been the problem?" says I as he switched off the engine.

"The bloody exhaust pipe won't stay in its place and consequently I had to take it off. For the past twenty minutes I have had the entire exhaust fumes blowing in my face. I stopped

157

twice and puked my guts out but I've got the hang of driving it alright."

Poor sod, I thought to myself, as we walked over to join the other two. Patrick then retold the story of his epic drive and enjoyed his pint. After a good half an hour's rest Mickey moved the Fergie across the intersection and tightened the exhaust pipe properly. Patrick was on his way again.

He arrived about twenty minutes later without further problems and in a much better mood.

"A job well done" we both told him. "Congratulations."

I have been trying to get Patrick to learn to drive for the past twelve years – perhaps he will now realise its time to do so. Imagine this day and age and not being able to drive? Stupid and selfish in my book – but then I am only his Dad!

That completed the second part of our week's project. Now all we had to do was clean her down and prepare her for spray painting.

I decided to name her *Jemima* and her number plate would be LS2002. She is a historic lady. The first tractor to grace the island, or lets say "she will be the first tractor to work the island." All being well. Please God. This was Spring 2002, already the wettest and most stormy year for eons.

It had been a stunning day, early August, and what else should we expect? From early sunrise the sky had been a lightly tinted azure with warmth aplenty exuding from a bright slightly yellow balloon, that slowly spanned the arc above. After lunch, however, a northerly breeze had arisen and lots of little white horses galloped down our western shore.

Shirley had been working on the wall since after tea, and I on the fence around the homestead. It had to be made more rabbit proof if anything was to survive. That morning Oscar had chased one rabbit from under a pile of corrugated sheets stored next to the kitchen. I witnessed the rabbit jump three foot off the ground escaping through the netted sheep wire that lined fifty percent of the surround. I couldn't believe my eyes but it was true. If one could jump out then it made sense that it could equally adeptly do the reverse. What chance had my shrubs and trees? Not much, so I set about barricading, even further, their likely escape routes.

We had agreed to call it a day at 6.00pm. Shirley was on her way down the hill when I heard her shout. I, at first, thought she was hailing Oscar but after repeatedly hearing my name I rushed out of the store room, where I was returning tools at that moment to see what was the matter.

"*Sophia* has broken her mooring and is drifting away," she said as she stared out westward. I rushed to her and we quickly made a plan. She dropped her tools and I put Oscar away into the cottage.

Shirley went down ahead of me to make ready the dinghy. She had just finished inflating it when I arrived and took the outboard down to the water's edge propping it against a tall rock.

We then carried out the dinghy, attached the outboard and pushed out into a slight surge. There was a lot of kelp around and it was difficult trying to paddle through it.

Shirley tried the engine and after four pulls got it started only for it to get tangled in the kelp and stall. It was impossible to get it restarted. The tide was going out and we were being pulled and dragged south westwards by it. I kept paddling away from the rocks as Shirley tried in vain to restart her precious little engine that normally started on first or second attempt. I even tried it a number of times but to no avail.

We tried our radio again and again but couldn't get a response. In the heat of the moment nothing seems to work. Murphy's law in action once again?

Sophia was fast disappearing into the sunset out towards Hook Head. We were now half a mile down southwest of our mooring. We decided to land amongst some very large rocks which might shield us from the outward surge.

A PINCH OF SALTEE

"I'll go up to the cottage and use the mobile to alert someone if you stay here with the dinghy. I shouldn't be too long."

"OK by me. We'll be beached soon anyway as the tide is running fast here," replied a wet and worried loved one. I kissed her lovingly prior to making a hasty retreat up the shore and then the quite stiff incline of the grassy ridge.

Back at the cottage I put the mobile to good use. Many calls were made in the next ten to fifteen minutes before I finally got hold of Declan's wife Alysia, who was herself, trying to make contact with him. She would have him phone us immediately she found him. She was sure he would jump into Tapaidh and set off for us straight away.

Meantime a number of the fishermen, whose cell numbers I had, rang me back but to little avail as they were miles out beyond the big island and another was across the bay off The Kirocks They all said they would keep an eye out for Sophia but wouldn't be returning for another hour or so. 'Good luck anyway and they would keep in touch later on'. Both Bobby and Mickey were miles away from Kilmore Quay on jobs and couldn't return.

Declan got back to me after a further ten minutes – I had now been away from Shirley for over half an hour. He was in the marina and would be out by our mooring in fifteen minutes. I wished him God speed.

Shirley arrived at the cottage in a terrible state of frustration, fear and exhaustion. I quickly poured us both a double Glenfiddich – a present from a recent visitor. Much appreciated!

We stood on our back porch (unfinished) and tried to find *Sophia* in the setting sun, out towards Hook Head. But not a ripple or even a smudge on the placid water of Ballyteighe Bay could we garner. The sunset was mesmeric but the occasion horrific.

We changed out of our wet clothes and awaited Declan's arrival. Plotting his course was easy in such still golden waters. Our radio miraculously sprang to life so we were able to keep in touch and direct him out beyond the eastern tip of the big island.

160

A PINCH OF SALTEE

We heard nothing for a long twenty minutes as Tapaidh passed close to us and then veered off into the still of the evening.

Crackle, crackle, hiss, hiss, crackle – "can you hear me Henry? I can see her and will be alongside in a few minutes. All seems ok."

"Great news, Dec."

Next time we heard from him he was already within our viewing range and *Sophia* surfed spectacularly in tow behind Tapaidh.

The sunset painted a golden canvass on waters heaving from the turbo charged throb of a homeward rescue team.

When they reached our mooring area Declan dropped another anchor and buoy. We watched with joy in our hearts. We thanked him profusely by shouting from the shoreline. It would be payback time in Kehoe's next time we came ashore.

"All part of the service," he laughed across the hundred metres between mooring and land.

It was now nearly 8.00pm. We then walked the half mile down the western shore and carried the dinghy up above the high water line and left it next to where Shirley had stacked the outboard. This was an area of enormous rocks – not some place one would want to be shipwrecked on.

We decided to leave both items there overnight and then carry them up to our normal landing area in the morning. Hopefully we would be more relaxed and over the worry of the proceeding three hours.

The barbecue in the boma that night tasted better than ever before. We finished a bottle of good red wine and devoured far too much Tandori chicken. We had a reason to be grateful for the way the adventure turned out.

It was only next day we came to realize how lucky we actually had been. Fate was very much on our side yet again. For, just imagine, if we had started the outboard and set off in pursuit of *Sophia*, and not being able to find her, had run out of fuel, what then? We didn't have our mobile with us and the radio was not working. I hate to think where we would have landed up. And Oscar was locked up in the cottage!

We were still very much on 'that learning curve' but it had better be put right without any further charades like these. A big block lettered message went into my mental notebook. Life was still too good to throw away so stupidly.

Saturday, September 20th 2002 was a day I treasured. Out for the first time came my daughter and grandchildren – they had arrived from South Africa two months previously and had already organized a house to live in and schools for Dougie and Claire.

Theirs had been a big decision. Leaving Africa where Deirdre (Dee Dee) was born, reared, married and had, until now, raised her family. Robert had already found himself a good job in Dublin and had been involved in the previous year's work with both Patrick, Mickey and the KQ gang.

The family, when in Natal, South Africa, had seen photo albums and a video taken by Patrick, of the island, their heritage. I hoped they too had the pioneering spirit of their grandpa. Otherwise our efforts might be for naught?

Declan brought them out in his spanking new launch *An Crosán* (Razorbill). Dee Dee is not the greatest sailor, she freely admits, but Robert and the kids absolutely adored the size and speed of the boat. When resident in Durban they did a lot of offshore fishing in their own boat.

Shirley collected them in two jaunts. It was flat calm. Robert and Claire came in first with most of the kit, to be greeted by a swimming Oscar acting as outrider.

I knew the family missed their dogs and horses so very much. Oscar had been showered with love and affection by them since their arrival in Dublin. He took them off later that morning, over the hills and showed them every inch of the farm. It was quite an adventure. Dee Dee went off on walks by herself. She was still trying to come to terms with their great move and culture shock, I felt. They had never been out of Africa – South Africa was their home.

Robert's family – mother, father, brother, sisters and cousins were still there. Here in Ireland Dee Dee and crew now had two extended families to fill the gap. Hopefully this would help to develop their future.

Never missing a chance for assistance in farm chores, we all got stuck into erecting a larger collecting area fence outside the crush corral. We banged in fence poles, pulled out lengths of sheep wire and erected it around a half an acre which ran up fifty meters of Shirley's wall and across to the northern end of the ruin (original homestead).

In stretching the wire, one end retracted hastily onto Shirley's hand and jammed her middle finger of her left hand. Very painful at the outset it gradually wore off. However, next day in Dublin, I took her into hospital to have it looked at. Her tendon was severed and it needed a splint which remained for six weeks. After that the finger was slightly out of kilter, to put it mildly, but quite usable. She was back typing almost immediately. She's tough – as if we didn't know.

That night, after a magical braai in an atmosphere almost African, the sleeping quarters were put to good use. Dee Dee and Robert bedded down in our 'guest room' and the children with us in the cottage.

This was how I had always envisaged it to be – for the use of both families, Shirley's and mine.

Claire lit the big candle early on so when we decided to turn in, that very special fantasia of light, filled the room. Dougie had the single bed and Claire a camp bed.

I kept the final magical touch for the last moment – it was my secret.

With Shirley and the family looking out over the cottage's half door, into the gloming of a still night, I pulled the cord of the generator and 'little saltee' we had electricity. The cottage and buildings became enveloped in a halation of light from a discretely

A PINCH OF SALTEE

placed Halogen globe donated by son Patrick. A pity he wasn't there to witness yet another historical event.

Some weeks later Bobby Stafford told us about his amazement as he also bore witness to that event. He was fishing out late along St. Patrick's Bridge. It evidently gave quite an aura to the place. And most satisfying for me to hear such a comment.

Next day was the annual visit from Dan Gubbins, our vet. This was the time of year to have the herd checked for TB and brucellosis

Bobby brought out Mickey and Dan late on the Sunday morning. Dee Dee was already painting, in brilliant red, the three gates into, out of and within, the corral and crush pens. The children were searching the shoreline for interesting flotsam. Robert, Shirley and I were finishing off the new collecting area.

Once the trio had arrived we all took off for a walk around the island to find and then herd the cattle homeward.

My greatest joy was that the new collecting area actually worked. All fourteen cattle were easily driven into it and once the concertina gate was closed, all remained without any hassle.

Usually we have big problems with Buttercup. She is so insistent on doing the opposite to all the rest. We can get her calf inside but with untold difficulty, herself. We had foxed her this time and she went through without any trouble.

Dehorning of the calves takes place at the same time. Dan manages to complete the entire task within an hour.

"With a great crush pen it makes handling the animals mighty easy. And with these two" pointing to Mickey and Bobby "my job is a pleasure," remarked Dan over the picnic table and some refreshment.

He was fascinated to hear Robert and Dee Dee's description of the same procedure in South Africa. We always savour the banter, both instructive and hysterical, on each of these annual visits. We really look forward to them.

It also means that, once the results are cleared, we can export to the mainland whatever animals are so designated.

A PINCH OF SALTEE

"I'm always thrilled to see the herd in such fine condition. There must be a rake of great minerals and vitamins in your soil, Henry."

"Long may it last, Dan," I replied with trepidation, as 2002 and had been such a wet year I was worried about the lack of late growth in the pasture.

The intrepid trio left us at about 3.00pm when Bobby took them off fishing behind the big island. They raced past, a couple of hours later, on their return to the mainland, hopefully with the evening's meal.

We had already put the family aboard *An Crosán* for their return to Dublin. It was such a great thrill for me to have had them resident for a couple of days. Now the next generation of Nicholsons and Grattan Bellew/Stevensons had witnessed and felt the Saltee experience. A most important factor in my mind. Another piece of the jigsaw fell into place.

Dan had earlier remarked on how much milk the cows carried. We chatted briefly about making cheese and using them more for our own use – about having one as 'a house cow' for instance. And that leads me on to another amusing tale.

When Mickey was assembling our new roof on the cottage he brought out a couple of helpers for four days. Either we would collect them or Declan would bring them on his routine run in the mornings. We, however, invariably returned the team in the evening. I would then give Mickey a list of food items to collect fresh from Hogan's shop on the following morning.

This day he somehow forgot to check the box of goodies with the list. So when it was mid morning tea break we discovered there was no milk. We do keep powdered substitute but quick as a flash he shouted down from the roof top "why not milk one of the cows. That's what they're there for, isn't it?"

"You are quite right, my bright hero," I replied as I beckoned Shirley to hear the solution.

"I'm up for it if you are," and with that we set off to bring the herd in. We had three suckling mothers so availability was not a problem.

Once in the crush, and we crammed three cows into it this time, I called for Mickey to help.

Shirley went for a large saucepan. I clamped Oulough Abbey tightly into the vee gate while Mickey caught hold of her tail and turned it up over her back. This helps to keep the animal quiet. These cows had never been hand milked.

Shirley had also brought a bucket of warm water and a cloth which I used to clean down and sooth the udder. Abbey remained remarkably docile as Shirley, reaching through the bars of the side panel, milked her – first the forward two teats and then the aft two. I couldn't believe how good the cow's behaviour was. But then again all I had to do was remember Ms. Hilliard's sound words to me "they become very tame if you show them affection and they are great milkers."

When the saucepan was nearly full I suggested we had enough. I needed to give Abbey some nuts to show it wasn't an ordeal as such – and that it was actually a happy and hassle free experience. One she wouldn't mind doing again, perhaps!

Shirley, I'm positive, was much more gentle than her calf. Perhaps Abbey was now to become our house cow for future emergencies or even availability on a regular basis.

Her milk lasted us three days. I had delight in scooping off the inch of thick yellow cream each morning and adding it to my cereal. Sinful, I know.

"Are you there" came wafting down from above. That meant upstairs in Shirley's office in Dublin. The question travelled down the powdered blue carpeted stairs, turned right in the hall and then first left through a closed door into our drawing room. I was sitting by the window doing the Irish Times crossword cushioned into my old oak spindle chair.

"I am indeed. What's the matter?" I shouted back.

"Come up please".

I found Shirley gazing into her Dell PC. There was a weather map across the screen.

"I think there's a break between two lows on Saturday or Sunday. That means we will have a calm spell with little or no winds. Maybe we can get out and get the calves off".

"How sure are you – are they?" said I quizzically.

"Well I can't be sure, you know that, but it looks good".

It had been such a frustrating year. Storm after storm, all westerly and nothing but rain, rain, rain. There had been very few chances to get stock, or anything, on or off the island.

But this was all I needed. I took the phone, returned to my chair and commenced organising everybody for the weekend. Few can realise how much planning went into an operation of this magnitude. It was essential to have everything at one's fingertips. Fortunately we had built up and cemented true friendships in Kilmore Quay Parish.

Mickey said he would take care of labour. He mentioned half a dozen names who I knew would assist if available. I said I would organise *the banana boat* and hopefully get Dave to be 'on duty' as well. I left it that I'd keep in touch re whether it would be Saturday or Sunday. But, and this was the critical factor I emphasised – everyone had to be on the Quay by 10.00am. That would give us five to six hours to do the job. And the job was to catch and bring off all the calves – five to six in total.

We had found, over the years, that most of the people of Kilmore Quay, bless them, did not respect time as much as we did. We had to be totally reliant on tides. Mickey cut through my thoughts. He guaranteed they would be there on time. Good for him

We had put a lot of thought into how best to utilise the island's off spring. One thing was painfully certain – they had to come off at three/four months of age. Any older they would be getting too heavy and too hard to handle. This crop, unfortunately, were a little older but I still thought they would be manageable. Please God I would be right.

Mickey had organised his friend Paddy Barry with his lobster boat to be ready for us. He brought a mutual friend Kevin. Our 'old reliable' Bobby, who had been involved in the first off take of calves the previous year, together with two youngsters Jack and Nigel made up their team. Shirley decided to leave it to the men.

Dave could not come out but gave us the use of *the banana boat,* in which my son Patrick, son-in-law Robert and I immediately followed the lobster boat *Leonora Jacinta* as they departed. Within about three minutes our engine cut out. Patrick said he knew what the problem was and loudly cursed Dave for not having fixed it. Evidently it had acted similarly when they took out the hay six weeks previously. Pat and Robert tried to fix it. All the problem was the lack of an O ring on the little clip that forged the link between petrol pipe and engine. Dave had tried also to mend it, with some sort of resin, but that obviously had not worked.

After three such stoppages we frantically waved clothes, shouted and created mayhem hoping that at least one person on Paddy's boat would see us in difficulties. He wasn't too far ahead of us so somebody did luckily see these gesticulations and had him turn back. Paddy then took us in tow. Just before leaving the harbour we watched the *Mary Margaret* lifeboat being launched and set off on its routine training exercises. I got a brainwave – a cheeky one. I phoned Dave from my mobile and caught him driving home outside the village.

"Dave, can you see out into the bay by any chance?" I asked.

"No not from here. What's the problem?"

A PINCH OF SALTEE

"Pity you can't see us. We are being towed by the lifeboat. We feel very stupid and let down." I put a lot of anger and feeling into those words.

"You're not! Oh my God. I'm sorry. I'll turn around and come back down to the harbour."

"No need to. We are being taken out to our mooring, thank you. You can settle the bill!" I reiterated with anger in my voice.

"Oh God no! I'm so sorry. How will you manage?" I could hear he was worried so I tightened the screw a little further. "Sorry is not good enough chum. Pat says you knew the engine was faulty. How could you do this to us. I thought you were a friend. That's all a thing of the past now I'm afraid. Thanks for nothing," and I hung up.

I had just managed to keep a straight face and from guffawing down the line. We broke into hoots of laughter. The three of us enjoyed the joke. We wondered what Dave would be doing right then. The bollocks!

Luckily we had the *Leonora Jacinta* towing us so we were safe and she could do the same for our return trip. We had six good humoured mates with us so we knew we were on a winner.

On board *the banana boat* was a new hayrack I had bought at the Bridgetown Co-op recently and had its size expertly increased by my welding fundi George Culleton.

This we carried up and placed inside the newly roofed cattle shed. Paddy and Kevin and the two lads accompanied me up the farm to collect and herd the cattle back to the homestead. They had brought a couple of shotguns hoping to bag a haul of rabbits and a cock pheasant or two. This would be part of my 'payback' package for their assistance.

Cattle were put in the collecting pens with the calves in the crush. Each calf was then caught and haltered. A strong rope was attached to the halter and then tied around its head and neck. This allowed for two men either side to hold and guide it down the hill and over the rocks to the awaiting *banana boat*. Once there all the team gently lifted the animal up and over the side placing it on a

169

bed of sacking. Sash cords were used to tie its legs. Once this was completed and the others had joined it they remained remarkably quiet throughout the voyage.

Best part of the entire operation was the machine gun rat tat tat of brash banter or accumulative craic that enveloped the team from crush to boat. Bobby Stafford, the tight lipped but fast fiendish fellow of 'ef' words reigned tall above the clouded linguistic largesse.

"The fecker – me ankle's crushed – the feckin whore – grab her there – not there yer ejeet – I'm holding her here – keep her head up – oh jeysus me toes is feckin crushed now"

"Will ye ever give over and hold her tight – like the mot you had out the other night, Bobby" broke in Mickey.

"Now leave her feckin out of it. Jesus Christ can't you keep her straight. Me back's broken – mind that feckin rock its sharp – Jesus Henry how many more of these feckers have you?"

"Oh cool it Bobby will yer" interjected Paddy who was on the opposite side to him doing the same job without the anecdotal injections.

"Jesus, you haven't got tonsillitis, I'm feckin suffering something brutal. Christ my foot is now crushed flat. Can't feel me toes or anything."

"Lucky that's all you can't feel", added Kevin.

This sort of torrential tirade, and much more to boot, lasted for the seven to ten minutes of each calf's two hundred metre journey down to embarkation. And it didn't stop there either. The camaraderie of these fisher farm folk is deep like the fathoms they trawl a living from.

Bobby had brought a large covered trailer down to the quayside earlier that morning. It was into this we loaded the calves. Untying or in fact the movement of any type of stock on the slipway, always attracted a large audience and this was no exception.

Once the ropes were loosened from their limbs it took a few minutes for the blood to flow back into circulation. The calves were so gentle, sweet and cuddly at that stage and were admired by the crowd.

Off they then went to Mickey's farm where a shed, hay, water and beef nuts were awaiting them. A great new experience

An hour later all nine of us gathered at the Upper Deck restaurant where Deirdre looked after us with a belated but sumptuous Sunday meal washed down with bottles of red and white wine.

The best part of the day for us, that is Pat, Robert and I, was when Paddy rose to thank me on behalf of the team, and cheerfully acclaimed it 'a great success. And when were they wanted next?' I thought to myself how does one measure friendship. This is the sort of close knit rural and fraternal philosophy that remains thankfully in the twenty-first century. Like harvesting and the collecting of haycocks in the old days. Everyone in the parish rallied round to bring them in. Fisher folk are quite secretive and introvertish but are deep bottomless men who stick together when stormy waters – of any kind – appear. The combination of fisher-farmer makes a doubly sound investment in friendships. We had experienced this gift yet again. We were blessed.

During the last moments of summer sunshine in 2002 we decided on buying a new boat. It wasn't anything to do with her recent escape but *Lady Sophia* had done us proud. She, like so many of the items to do with the project, was also bought as an experiment. We were so lucky having run with our gut feeling from the start. Her 15 HP Evinrude outboard had given little trouble and, although a mite too heavy for the two of us to carry, had provided enough power when needed.

Sophia herself had transported sheep, calves, cement, trees, shrubs and many other items as well as being the perfect people carrier.

A PINCH OF SALTEE

Her faults were few, mainly structural, as we found out over a four year period. We sped through some high seas, got a sound thrashing around in her, and took on a volume of water at times worryingly dangerous.

We didn't need anything bigger in length but having a broader beam would be safer, stronger and more stable. The local fishermen kept telling us we needed something beamier.

Patrick had palled up with someone at work who supplied his site with filtration tanks. During the course of conversation, boating came up as the site he was working on was in Poolbeg, Dublin, the very heart of Dublin Bay. Martin Kennedy explained that he had a boatyard close by and a factory in Connemara. He made fibreglass boats of fifteen to twenty-three footers known as Malahide Workers alongside his filtration units.

On one Saturday morning during the winter Patrick took me along to meet Martin, his 'fibreman' Paul, and a look over their setup in the basin.

I was particularly impressed with their twenty-three footer but it would be too big for Shirley and I to handle. They then showed us a just finished 'fifteen' which we both fell for immediately. It looked twice the size of Sophia – and why? Because it had a beam, much wider and therefore more spacious than our *Sophia*.

I phoned Shirley straight away and told her about our find. She was thrilled to hear that we had found something so easily. Their usual products, however, didn't have cuddies – little half cabins up front like on *Sophia* – but Martin would design one especially for us. We found a cuddy essential for storing items whilst in transit and for the dinghy when deflated and its engine when packed away in its container between trips.

I was quite confident of reselling *Sophia* so when March 2003 arrived I placed an advertisement in *Buy and Sell*. Unknown to me the paper now came out three times a week.

At 08.30 on a Monday morning I took a call from a Michael Bolger who had seen the advertisement that instant. We

172

discussed *Sophia* in great detail and he ended by saying "hold her for me – I'll be around at 5.30pm this evening after work to see some photos of her." I agreed.

That afternoon whilst entertaining a friend from South Africa and leafing through photo albums of the island, the door bell rang.

"I'm Michael Bolger. I'm an hour early but is it ok to see the photos?"

"Yes, of course, do come in."

Our coffee table was awash with photos so he not only saw some of *Sophia* on dry land but also at work off our mooring in varying seas.

He liked what he saw, took out his wallet and handed over a hefty down payment on my asking price.

"Would I please bring her up from Kilmore Quay and deliver her to him?" He lived not a stone's throw away in an adjoining estate. A small world.

We delivered her the following week to a happy Michael who was retiring at month's end.

His signature tune would be 'gone fishing'– off and around Dalkey island as his retirement hobby and relaxation. *Lady Sophia*, we felt, would have a loving owner.

Meantime *LS Bluebell* was taking shape in Connemara and would be ready for launching mid April. She would be powered by a new 15 hp Mariner four stroke outboard, and should, hopefully, give us endless joy in the years ahead.

The winter of 2002/03 was an exacting six months for buildings and animals on the island. Too much rain throughout the spring and summer months had curtailed late growth of grasses. This meant we were in for a rough time ahead. We had to make emergency plans

A PINCH OF SALTEE

During October Patrick, Liezel and Robert spent a weekend down on the island whilst we took a week's holiday in the South of France. The weather was kind to them, so they managed to bring out two piled loads of hay on *the banana boat*.

This they stacked into two halves of the circular metal hay feeder which was already placed inside our newly roofed portion of the original farm house. The hay would be stored until we decided there was no more grass. All we had to do then was to open ten metres of fencing and the stock would have free access to the fodder. We reckoned we would do this late January and there should be enough bales to see them through until the new growth in April.

All cattle and sheep were alive and well when we counted them late January.

What a surprise it was to find we were two Kerries short a month later. We searched the island thoroughly but nothing – not even a carcass or two.

The two missing cattle were our bulls – Knockane Uinseann and Millennium Patrick. An enigma of giant proportion.

My only solution to the mystery was that they had fought each other and fallen over the cliffs, onto the jagged rocks below and had then been battered to a pulp by the raging seas. It had been a stormy few months.

We had lost a couple of calves in this way previously and Millennium Patrick, as already mentioned, had almost lost his life on the rocky foreshore.

This would mean I had to import another young bull. I would put this off, however, until a later year as I felt the foundation cows needed a rest. They had been wonderful producers for their first three seasons.

We hadn't been prepared for that loss and we certainly were not ready for another. But it came. This time in the form of a freak accident.

The new roof on the hay shed had not had its concrete barges placed along the sides or across the top. Patrick had made a fine job of building up the side walls so that no westerly winds – our prevailing ones – could get under the roof. Bad weather had left no time to properly finish the cement work. This is an endless struggle.

In our naivety, however, we did not realise that storm force 8 from the south would rush through the only entrance and lift the 24 sq. m roof just enough to allow it to slide down to the ground below – a distance of approximately 4 m. Nothing was broken.

Two Kerries, however, must have been sheltering behind the shed when the storm struck and were hit and therefore trapped beneath the roof end.

It was a tragic ending to a long winter. One of these fatalities was 001, Saltee Little Lady – our first born. This meant we had lost both our original Kerry calves, Lady and Patrick.

When I showed Mickey the damage he fortunately said it wasn't a hassle.

"Give me a few strong men and once I have stripped off the sheets we'll be able to replace the roof. This time I'll get George to cut me some iron bars and clip the beams to the stonework. The building will have to fall down to move it. These storms are fierce awful out here. Never seen or heard anything like it."

I loved his optimism.

"Roll on the summer and a belt of high pressure. Sure we'll get the whole lot re-roofed then, eh Mick?"

"Sure, we'll try anyhow."

Chapter Ten

Bluebell – Death and Destruction – Robert, Grandchildren –
Tenda – Hornies off – Bannon Show - Sick Prank

"Come along and see the hull", came from the dulcet tones
of boat builder Martin Kennedy. This was mid March, 2003.

Shirley and I went to his boatyard in Dublin basin and saw
the bones of a hull resplendent amongst a few of her larger and
beamier siblings. All had been transported up from his Connemara
factory. Even in this naked viewing she looked a lot bigger than
Sophia.

Shirley showed where she wanted cleats, lockers and the
mooring roller. The cuddy could be built from bow to just in front
of the forward bench. This we felt would be adequate to store all
our necessities.

Martin said it would be ready to launch in mid April. That
suited us just fine as we were about to spend ten days in the South
of France. We were hoping to see the sun and get enough Vitamin
C into our bodies prior to what we hoped would be a successful
summer on the island.

On the drive home and during a walk on Sandymount
strand with Oscar, names were discussed. We decided on *Bluebell*
as the island was famous for its blue sheen and slightly scented
crop every May/June. We also ordered a new Mariner 15 horse 4-
stroke engine from Martin who imported them as a service for his
various clients.

On our return from France *Bluebell* was not ready but was
promised the following week!

Martin delivered her without engine – still in transit? – to
Kilmore Quay and we were joined by Mickey, Paddy and Bobby
for the launch.

We clamped our little 4-horse Yamaha onto her and gave
Bluebell her maiden voyage around the harbour – in a very

blustery wind. We made it, with difficulty, to our berth and tied her up.

The KQ3 gang gave her the 'thumbs up'. The design and beam would make it easier for us to handle they agreed. We looked forward now to the engine's arrival and many months of successful boating ahead.

Mariner 15 arrived the following week but it then took a further fortnight to find a soft enough day for a trip out and around the island. There was too heavy a surge to land but we could see some of the herd. We had two new calves, and the flock of sheep had some lambs. Growth of new grass didn't look too promising but the animals did have heads down and the youngsters were gamboling about the place.

Both *Bluebell* and Mariner performed to our satisfaction. We were relieved.

It took another six weeks before we managed to put to sea again.

I constantly ask myself "are our summers (one could say what summers?) getting shorter?" Our problem, as you will have realised, is not rain or sun but wind. 2003, excepting for a couple of weeks in spring, had been a sky full of storms – right up 'till mid summer.

It was Friday, 13th June when we managed to land with safety. There was a light southerly breeze which unfurled the flag and showed that the storms had pushed the flag pole slightly out of perpendicular. We kept an eye on the flag from 10.30am 'till 2.30pm when Shirley decided the surge was getting quite strong. It was two hours before high tide so we launched the dinghy from our little sandy beach and returned to the mainland.

In those few halcyon hours, the first time since early spring, we cleaned out all the rooms, aired the cushions, opened all doors and windows, started the fridge and had lunch.

Shirley strimmed the haggard area which was sprouting ragwort. It was wonderful to find our shrubs had all survived the winter and our resident rabbit colony. Everything was shooting and some were flowering.

We then came upon the horrors of absentee farming under stormy conditions. Four cattle were missing. We found one skeleton on the shoreline below the homestead, another halfway along the shore to the south, and quite a number of bones over near Smugglers Cove. We hadn't been able to land safely since March.

Some of the cattle, most probably, fell over the cliffs in foraging for better grass. Or they had all wandered down on to the rocky shoreline and became entrapped by the incoming tide. As 2003 has had months of storms and raging violent seas it would be easy for them to perish in such a way. What a loss, but luck was with us as we had moved most of our heifer calves to the mainland in January. Parts of cliff sides had subsided and erosion along the shoreline was enormous.

This was the first winter we had lost animals.

Three Kerry cows, however, were fat, sleek and well. Two had new calves. Horny, my 'leader of the herd' obviously was the first to calve as her bull calf was a lot bigger than the second. Both of these were sired by Millennium Patrick.

The sheep flock had increased by three lambs with hopefully more to follow. They were coated with heavy fleeces and we wondered how we would manage to herd them indoors for shearing in July. The flock were still desperately wary of humans after last season's fiasco with the 'mad dog' episode so they now took off at a fast pace to escape every time they saw a human. They knew Oscar and, as he didn't approach them, wasn't an unsettling factor.

After shearing, the flock would be sold off and taken to the mainland for sale.

In their place would arrive the first consignment of SOAY sheep who should be ideal island inhabitants.

A PINCH OF SALTEE

Emanating from the island of the same name off the north coast of Scotland they are recognised to be the oldest breed of sheep in Europe. They have lived for thousands of years on various islands, are virtually immune from disease, eat little and shed their own fleeces annually. And are an endangered species and a rare breed.

I had endeavoured to source them some five years before this but was unable to.

Quite by chance Shirley and I were visiting a fellow Kerry cattle breeder in Co. Wexford in May of this very year, 2003. On returning from inspecting his excellent herd we passed along the fence of his neighbour and there I spotted some strange little animals that reminded me of Soays. I remarked on the fact and the reply "indeed they are", said our host. "He has nearly fifty of them so if you should want some, I am sure he will accommodate you. I'll set up a meeting for you."

And that was how we found an energetic well cared flock of this endangered species. They lived in the rarefied air of an academic world and were together with some South American Rea, part of this retired scholar's rare breeds hobby.

They look like a cross between a deer and a small goat. Their lambs are extremely faun like. They are only eighteen inches high and the rams can grow quite large curled horns.

The island's environment should be perfect as this way of living is inherent in them. It will make our lives a lot easier and they should fit in with their new companions – a first shipment of Fallow deer.

Shirley and I have taken the decision to keep our three original Kerry cows and move the calves each year to the mainland, to a leased piece of land near Duncormick, not far from Kilmore Quay.

Our stocking of the island has always been an experiment. We wished to upgrade the pastures and utilise the acreage to its best advantage. That has been partly achieved with sheep and cattle minimising the bracken growth. Soays and Fallow deer should hopefully carry this on. And both will look quite majestic on the skyline.

Kerries are the ideal cattle for the island and we would maintain a full herd if we were twenty years younger. But wintering is a problem, even with an abundance of hay and self feeders as we have on offer. The mechanics of transporting fodder, and cattle, on an annual basis, proved too much of a hassle for us. And hassles we do not want.

We have enough Saltee blood in both male and female lines of our Kerry herd to keep it prominent in the years ahead. Perhaps a grandson will take on the responsibility and privilege of farming the island full time? We would love that or perhaps we will have to return to the days of tenant farming?

I had the feeling that we were going to have a 'super' summer, one like I remembered growing up many moons ago. We prayed for a change in the weather.

"It had to come", I kept saying to myself. And it did within the period of the next two months.

The shortest night followed by the longest day – June 20th and 21st 2003, saw us experience both delights out on the island.

Shirley and I went out on Friday, 20th, a beautiful day and the first for many weeks, i.e. no wind with high pressure. We brought out a full load on *Bluebell* who plied her way under some weighty freight. Things like cattle nuts, dozens of plants, cool boxes and many presents for the cottage given at Christmas and birthdays by members of the family.

My son-in-law, Robert, with my grandchildren, Dougie and Claire, were arriving next morning so we had plenty of help to clean up the entire haggard, boma and surrounding area. Shirley set about strimming the path down to the shore, the collecting paddock and the next section of wall that she would restore. We noticed that bracken was late in maturing but nettles were about to flower.

A PINCH OF SALTEE

The clearing and maintenance of paths for stock movement is an item that will be included in our annual REPS return. The restoration of walls will be an ongoing task as whatever is restored one year could well be, and is, knocked during ensuing winter months.

A lot of repair work was needed on the collecting paddocks' fence. I decided to order metal stanchions and phoned George Culleton requesting him to make me up two dozen 10ft. strong angle iron stakes with holes drilled every foot from the top.

With deer and soays coming in the next month this fence had to be eight feet tall to fence the former. This little paddock would now be known as the deer pen.

The boys cleaned out the boma whilst Claire assisted me in re-potting and planting out trees, shrubs and plants. It was great to see the honeysuckle, twin climbing roses, jasmine and how all the various geraniums and hydrangeas had successfully weathered the winter and were now taking off, some in bloom.

The clump of willow had also survived and the four birches were shooting out dainty green sprigs of delight.

My South African oak tree had been 'got at' by the rabbits once again, and although alive was now well stunted. A liberal dressing of rich compost was immediately applied.

The two original fuchsia bushes, brought from Kerry with the heifers, were in full bloom. Why the rabbits hadn't eaten them this winter remains a mystery?

On the evening of the longest day we held our first 'braai' of the year. Two plump mackerel, lamb cutlets and steak were cooked by Robert. On a fine balmy evening 'eating outside' is really the only way. Everything tastes so much better. Even the beer and wine dons a special flavour.

Robert and the kids played cards for another hour or so and then retired to bed, pleasantly exhausted. We had already turned in well ahead of them.

A PINCH OF SALTEE

On both mornings I had awoken at 04.30 and made my first 'cuppa' by 05.00. I plotted the day's activity and worked out the mechanics of it. Kitty Kallens song 'little things mean a lot' has always been one of my all time favourites and each morning waking to the shrill but melodic call of our resident jenny wren, then to be followed by cocky pheasant calling his harem, set each day in motion with joy in my heart. These meant 'a lot' to me.

Dougie cooked a fry for his family on Sunday after which the three of them went off exploring and photographing the nesting birds. Robert wanted to send the children, who were holidaying in South Africa the following week, with a full album of up-to-date for his parents who lived in Pietermaritzberg, Natal.

It was another memorable weekend. The children didn't want to return to Dublin but unfortunately Claire's school had not yet broken up.

That Sunday the island was being used as the turning point in a 'swim for Chernobyl' fund raiser. As we arrived into the marina the shoal of well greased swimmers were setting off on their perilous event, flanked on either side by a flotilla of RIBS in case of any problems. Fortunately there were none and a goodly sum was raised.

I am all for the island being used for such good causes and have been thrilled, over the years, to be told about school projects, which some of the children who have visited with us, had completed and won prizes with. Canoeists are becoming regular visitors, some of them camping over if we are in residence. It is so interesting to hear of their adventures.

Robert had two weeks leave from July 1ˢᵗ so the three of us set off once again for Kilmore Quay.

We had, on the previous day, been down to Western Marine in Bullock Harbour to look for a dinghy as a replacement for our inflatable. Our feelings were that a light boat with a hard bottom would be the answer. It had to be light enough for us to carry, that was the main criteria.

A PINCH OF SALTEE

They had a range of BIC (the pen makers) boats which seemed ideal. We tested the 252's weight and found we could handle it. We mulled it over through lunch and afternoon and having had no response from repeated calls to advertisements in 'Buy & Sell' we decided, over a piece of cake and cup of Lapsang, to 'go get her', which we did!!

Their excellent salesman, Tray, an American, who over the previous few years had assisted us in many nautical problems, attached it to the roof rack on *Humphrey* (our Mazda Demio). We named our new purchase *tenda* – she was bright orange with a white undercarriage. Still wrapped in its bubble pack and cellophane it looked like a gorgeous present about to be presented – it was, to us. And hopefully we would have many safe landings in her.

Next day Robert followed us down to Kilmore Quay, riding shotgun as it were. The trip, however, was uneventful and we launched *tenda* within minutes of arrival.

She towed well behind *Bluebell,* her catamaran hull skiing over the surf. We had an enormous load of varying goods and it was a joy for us to pile them onto *tenda's* solid frame. Our 4 hp outboard was ideal and although three trips were needed to transport the goods everything went swimmingly!

tenda was a success. The critical test was how well Shirley and I managed to carry her up and over the rocks. That, too, went without strain.

We, Robert and I, planned to stay out on the island for two weeks. We had a lot of work to see to and a major undertaking or three to carry out.

the banana boat was launched so we could now transport all the building and roofing material to finish the remainder of the buildings.

A PINCH OF SALTEE

Thirty joists (rafters) cut to length, thirty sheets of 12ft by 3ft 6ins iron sheeting and 400ft of laths came out in two trips over the next couple of days.

Paddy's *Leonora Jacinta* towed *banana* to our mooring with Mickey and Bobby then paddling her ashore. Their paddles were two pieces of the roofing timber!! Paddy remained on his boat letting out a length of rope attached to *banana*.

Shirley then paddled *tenda* out and collected him. The six of us made a line from *banana* to above the high waterline and within thirty minutes had the entire load carried up to safety.

This, and the next evening's cargo, was carried out on a rising tide – about two hours to high which meant that *banana* was on and above our sandy beach, rock free.

After a dozen Heineken and plenty of explosive craic the 'trendy trio' departed to return with another heavy load the following evening. One has to grab every opportunity in our favour to undertake and complete such safaris. Good weather, calm seas, high pressure made the perfect equation on these placid occasions. Now we needed another week of that recipe, together with a few willing souls, to assist Mickey in his endeavours.

Next day the three of us carted up sand for future cement work. We then concentrated on bringing in the small herd which we did and tagged the two bull calves, in the crush.

Amongst general farm maintenance we damned up 'Patrick's'. The wall had been somewhat trodden down and a dozen leaks had appeared. The spring was still pumping out a rich flow of clear water.

After Robert's return to Dublin, Shirley and I had another five glorious days in which time we – the two of us and Oscar – herded in our flock of sheep. This took an enormous amount of guile, patience and perseverance. We shut them into the crush pen area and offered them water and nuts as their B and B.

Next morning at 04.30 I inspected them and all seemed secure. But at 06.30 the 'cupboard was bare'!! One little adventurous lamb had wormed a way through my temporary barricade constructed between pen and outer wall. This led the rams to believe that they too could escape – which they duly did.

Shirley cried with anger and exasperation. It was all my fault. I had not done a thorough job. I had been caught unprepared for the flock's arrival. We were both distraught.

After an extremely quiet breakfast I set about tying, with heavy wire this time, my original structure. By the time I had finished not even a bull calf could bash through it – I hoped and prayed?

Sometime later we set out again to herd them back to base. This time we managed to lead them along strimmed paths, and despite being 'shooed' on by the cattle at one juncture, they behaved quite well until they got to the field above the homestead. There they split into two groups. However, luck was on our side yet again as Mickey had come out that morning and was working on the hayshed roof.

Mobile phones now came into their own and by communicating amongst the three of us we out flanked and out thought the flock. With a lot of patience and by a one step at a time approach we herded them all into the collecting area. During this drive Shirley's cell rang. It was deep in her short's pocket. Taking the call she found it was from her daughter Vicki in Bangalore, India.

"You sound out of breath Mum. What are you doing?"

"I'm actually running through heavy bracken trying to cut off a ewe and two lambs who have broken away from the flock."

They had their conversation and were thrilled to be in touch 'though world's apart!

We had, in the morning, strengthened the collecting area fence so were quite confident of holding them. Up until this point it had taken over an hour to drive and contain the flock. Now the three of us, with Oscar patrolling the outside of the fence behind us, very slowly urged them into the funnel which leads to the crush pen.

A PINCH OF SALTEE

One ram broke away through the semi-circle we commanded and bashing into the fence turned upside down landing on the top strands of wire and fell outside.

In that instance I said "don't panic. Let him go. Concentrate on the rest."

Sometimes you find a gem – not perhaps quite like Cecil Rhodes and the great hole at Kimberley a couple of centuries ago, but a little something that makes an endeavour worthwhile. It happened for us. That renegade ram, finding himself all alone, climbed onto Shirley's restored wall that ran along the southern side and jumped back over the wire fence. He joined up with the others who were now mesmerised by the gate and wouldn't enter through it. His momentum, however, carried them through and all the flock rushed along into the crush pen. We had bagged them all. Immediate preparations were put into motion. Paddy would tow out *the banana boat* in the morning with Mickey and Paul and we would carry the flock down, singly, each one tied and place them in the boat.

This went off with the minimum of fuss but with the usual dollop of high octane craic. They were taken to my little piece of leased land where Brian, the shearer, performed his duties next morning. They would then head to the Mart when the price was right.

the banana boat that morning, had brought out cement and our cement mixer which I had bought a year ago and was awaiting such an occasion for transportation. This was yet another historic piece of machinery. A first on the island. Another item that would make it much easier to build with.

Shirley, in her anxiety to cut off the flock from escaping across a certain area whilst on the second drive home, the morning before, had quite nastily cut her left shin on some rigid Ragwort stalks. Being the person she is, not a mention was made until I noticed profuse bleeding sometime later. She immediately bathed the area in the sea and rubbed it with seaweed. That night we cleansed it again, this time with Dettol and covered with Elastoplast.

Two days later it looked very raw and viciously septic. We decided to return to Dublin and see our doctor. He kindly dressed it and put her on antibiotics. It took a week to heal up. That makes three, if not four, permanent scars from island work!

Our doctor posed the question "why do you do it?" It's not that easily answered. I suppose 'because its there' is too hackneyed. But that's the truth of it. And it keeps us active in both body and mind. A most important factor when one is getting on in years. Imagine sitting around doing crosswords all day long? Eucch! We enjoy it. It is and has been from the outset a team effort. Perhaps some day someone will appreciate the island as we do and love it as much.

The 2003 Bannow Rathangan Agricultural Show on the wonderful farm owned by the Whites of Killag, Duncormick welcomed over 40,000 spectators on a fine sunny day – the first Thursday in July.

Three Saltee Little Kerry heifers were on show. They created a lot of interest, behaved well, loaded and unloaded up onto and from a trailer returning to my leased land in the evening.

One of the interested visitors to our stand was a Father Felix Byrne who is an agent for the Irish Charity, Bothar, which exports cattle and goats to third world countries in Africa. He was sending out a first consignment of in-calf Kerries this September. If successful in the next nine months then he may well order my heifer progeny for future exports.

I can't help feeling that there is a touch of divine providence in this as I would adore nothing better than my beloved 'little rascals' being tended by Malawi farmers in the continent I spent such a major portion of my life and love so much. It would be a sort of 'full circle' completion of aspiration. Something no one could have imagined at the outset of our island project. But something so fulfilling if realised. And I will be able to teach them Kiswahili!

After so much going right something had to bring life's reality into the foreground. And it came in trumps.

In a tragic accident in Biarritz, south-west France, Shirley lost her granddaughter Jan Nicholson. She was Shirley's son Tony's second daughter. He spends a holiday each August on the island. Tony and Etain are two very special people who had two lovely daughters and two sons. A very close knit unit loved and respected by all who know them.

This was a devastating loss – a tragic shortening of a beautiful girl's life so full of hope and charity. The outpouring of love and affection by such a wide grouping of the community before, at and after her funeral, bore witness to everything both Shirley, who knew her for her full twenty one years and me for ten years, had seen in her divine granddaughter. One cannot imagine the grief at losing ones child. I experienced part of that agony and comforted my darling as much as humanly possible.

During the last six years we have lost a few moorings with two anchors most probably "out there" somewhere beneath a bed of seaweed.

For this 2003 season we made a permanent anchorage with shackled mooring attached. Half a 44 gallon pvc drum was filled with concrete with a metal eye cemented in. This was given two months to mature before being taken out and dropped by hoist from Paddy's lobster boat.

The mooring ropes and buoy were shacked to a length of chain attached to the concrete drum.

This, believe it or not, lasted for just two months? On arriving out at the island in late June we could not find the brightly coloured buoy. It had been removed. Luckily we carry an anchor and so dropped it in the area our mooring is usually found.

A PINCH OF SALTEE

Our thoughts went to the possible ways this "permanent" could have been removed.

Perhaps it had been accidentally caught by a line of lobster pots and during their hauling in process had somehow broken the shackle. This seemed the most likely but was an improbable solution.

The lads who had manufactured the entire mooring were adamant that the shackle could not have been broken. It had to have physically – manually –been taken apart. And who would have been the dastardly one who contrived this pathetic joke – prank?

An hour after landing I found the mooring buoy and all its rope, but without the joining shackle. It was some one hundred yards south of our landing spot wedged, by the tides, between some rocks.

This made the enigma more enormous. Perhaps someone wanted the concrete anchor and hoisted it up onto their boat for replacing elsewhere and for their advantage?

On making enquiries in and around the harbour we learnt about some of the local politics and petty jealousies that abound. Up 'till now we have kept out of this and very much to ourselves. We have been assisted by many people in the past six years but some others seem jealous of those who have opted to assist us. Something quite foreign to us. It brings home the mysteries and myths of the squinting windows syndrome!

A great pity that this person should see fit to play childish pranks. Such a person will undoubtedly meet his comeuppance and watery Waterloo. We, however, wish whoever it was well. No hard feelings. There were no accidents or tragedies this time. Just don't try it again!

August continued to produce high pressure after high pressure. Calm seas allowed us to get cracking with all the building work – two of the KQ3 gang were available for two or three working 'bouts' each week. And it's amazing how much can be achieved when the will is there and the weather is fine.

189

A PINCH OF SALTEE

"Shirts off lads", and "lets get at it" was the slogan. It worked.

The stock cum hayshed was completed. Paddy's mastery of stone masonry even surprised himself. A door was fitted and windows filled with various ingredients, Perspex for light, wire mesh to prohibit access or escape and slatted timber for added ventilation.

Kerries, deer and soays can now access it during the winter and all self feeding fodder outlets will remain dry.

The more we work on these old buildings the more we want to restore them. Unfortunately both gable ends of this, the original house, are beyond repair. Perhaps, however, over the coming years it may be possible to knock them and rebuild?

The KQ3 gang seem to think it's possible. I have told them to proceed 'as they so desire'. Their obvious interest marries my passion. A recipe surely for certain success.

Fallow deer being loaded onto banana boat

A PINCH OF SALTEE

Chapter Eleven

Soays – Fallow Deer – Vet's Visit – Great Growth –
Cabot's Report – KQ3 Gang

My contact for the Soay sheep phoned to say he was leaving for London in seven days time. Could I possibly select and collect my bunch before that? I agreed we could and called Mickey to please accompany us. We set a date and he showed interest in buying a few for himself.

A flock of twenty odd had been cut from the complete number of nearly fifty and were in a separate paddock for our perusal.

This man really had done some research into layout of paddocks and pens with sheep fencing and smart galvanized gates leading off a main passage some 4 metres wide. Halfway down this collecting passage were two gates three metres apart. Once closed they offered a perfect pen from which to select, catch and carry away.

This time we were just selecting and would return in a couple of days with a trailer to transport them to their island domain.

We didn't take too long in choosing and catching the first seven. I chose two young rams and five yearling ewes but could find no more youngsters. I had especially stated I wished to purchase ewe lambs or hoggets and this had been agreed.

Not to cause a row I agreed to take a further three two-year-old ewes to fill my required number and then I said I was 'throwing' in another old ewe to balance the 'luck'! He wasn't too keen on that but I laughed it off and said I would be back with the cash to collect them in two days time.

On our return trip to Kilmore Quay we discussed the transaction and we came to the conclusion that 'we had been done' on the deal as I knew there were plenty more ewe lambs and hoggets in his total flock. Most of the group left out for us were young rams?

Two days later Mickey and Paddy accompanied us to the farm. We had great difficulty in herding, never mind catching, them – although two speeding lambs jumped straight into both Mickey's and my arms as we attempted to close them into the pen. These I dumped promptly in the trailer after tagging their ears. It took the four of us plus the farmer and his wife – both inactive and fairly elderly people – an hour to complete the task.

We were invited to partake in some refreshment which they kindly offered us. Cold beer went down well after such a hot operation!

On our way to the car and trailer I purposely asked to see the other flock. We were shown them and noticed that virtually all that year's lambs and yearling ewes made up the majority. There were only three rams running with them.

Our presumption had been correct and I displayed my disgust at his behaviour. I had grudgingly paid my money for a package not exactly the one I wanted.

I couldn't get away quick enough and will not be doing business there again.

That evening we loaded them onto the *Leonara Jacinta* with Shirley and I in *Bluebell* accompanying them.

We offloaded them into *tenda* with Shirley ferrying them to me on the shore. They travelled without hassle and looked so sweet, like china figurines, as I lined them up on the sand between rocks.

Oscar was totally immersed in their smell and intrigued by their horns. Although hobbled they showed enough aggression towards him when he approached. He thought it a great game.

Shirley and I carried them up to the crush pen and untied their roped legs. They lay still while the circulation proceeded through their veins and then casually strolled out into the newly created soay/deer pen where they stayed for three days bonding with their new surrounds.

I then opened the mesh gate without them knowing and without us herding them. They found it in their own good time and gracefully explored the pathway up and eastwards.

That night they returned of their own accord and slept in their winter quarters before departing again at 9.00 am in the morning.

Next day we prepared for the arrival of our four Fallow deer. Percy Podger had been the man doing the deal for me and he said he expected to arrive at Kilmore Quay at 18.30 hours.

I had requested Dave to assist with *banana boat* and if possible bring a strong friend to help carry the three wooden crates (1.5 metres x 1metre x 0.75 metres) they were contained in. When 7.00pm arrived and no Percy I got a call to say he was delayed for another hour? Nothing I could do so I suggested we repose to the newly reopened and refurbished Wooden House bar. This we did for the next hour and a quarter collecting 'friends' as the time passed. When Percy's arrival occurred at 8.30pm we had seven to assist with the offloading from trailer and onloading into *the banana boat*.

The crates were more awkward than heavy but with some expert tying of rope by Dave they were manoeuvred onto *banana boat*.

Out we went in convoy with us landing just ahead of them. It was now 10.00pm and getting dark. It had been my intention to release the deer into our newly constructed 8ft. high pen, letting them bond with the place like the Soays and then releasing them to pastures new

But when I looked at the size and weight of the crates I calculated how long it would take – if possible at all, over the rocks, etc. – I said the deer must be released on the shore. It was now 10.45 and dark. I was worried about the rocks and how the deer would react in handling them. We lifted each crate up a good thirty metres and placed them, one at a time, just in front of the sloping grass bank of the island hoping they would walk out, peer around, see the grass and head up the slope. Not on your life. The first lady walked out, peered about herself and took off, at a trot along the southern shoreline. Not a bit interested in going up the bank. Off she went into the gloming of a still, humid but starry night.

The second madam, despite Shirley placing herself on the southern shoreline route, did exactly the same as her colleague.

Finally we had the heaviest crate holding a stag and a hind. This was placed in position. We held our combined breath in anticipation.

This time they emerged, looked right, looked left, and headed NORTH also along the rocky shoreline. Murphy's Law in active drive!

There was nothing we could do about their whereabouts in the dark so we retired to the candle lit cottage and imbibed in well deserved liquid refreshment.

The merry band of Dave, his two children, Lewin and Molly, Percy, Sean, Pauline and Bodie departed the island at 11.45pm? Another historic event in the farm's evolution. And one enjoyed by all involved despite the hard backbreaking work.

"It was a magical evening, Henry" said Dave when I expressed by gratitude as we shoved *banana boat* out into the dark waters of the bay.

I knew his feelings at that moment as Lewin and Molly had been spun the story of watching Santa's reindeer being 'let out for a holiday on Henry's island before working at Christmas'.

The most telling remark of the evening came from Molly, sitting beside her brother on a big bench-like rock just to the right and south of the crates.

A PINCH OF SALTEE

"They are lovely but Rudolph didn't have a red nose. Why?"

How do you answer that one? My immediate and unrehearsed reply was "Oh they've come from a cold place Molly. Now they will get plenty of sun and Rudolph's nose will get burnt. Then it will be red like mine".

It seemed to satisfy her. Her query, however, brought back the well-known adage – never act with children or animals!

With both soays and deer now on the island another part of the jigsaw fell into place. There remained only two pieces for completion.

the banana boat was used with great regularity during this fine spell despite its outboard being vandalised while moored in the harbour. Another sick prank perhaps? Dave had to order various spares which took time to arrive. It was July before he found time to do some fishing with his children.

Paddy became adept at towing *banana boat* out and poling her onto our beach.

At times Shirley had to haul a rope out and attach it to the lobster boat. Sometimes she really battled the current as the one hundred metre rope curved away from *tenda* almost dragging it against the output of her little engine. But she always made it. A gem of a woman!

After completing the hayshed work, they commenced on the second cottage – Deer – with all timber work, rafters, joists and laths, going up in literally a few days work. They finished the roof on Saturday, August the 16th, the day after Dan Gubbins, our vet, had visited for his annual T.B., brucellosis testing and the dehorning of both bull calves. Ivan Ward, our Arthurstown farmer friend, also visited us on that day and assisted Dan in his deliberations.

A PINCH OF SALTEE

After an hour of veterinary work we walked the island and spotted the soays still in their new habitat. They had chosen Northfield which gently slopes and stretches down to the point at which St. Patrick's Bridge reaches Little Saltee.

Shirley put forward the idea that the grazing there could be quite similar to that from whence they came. Previously all other sheep had taken up residence on the southern slopes. Perhaps, when the bracken dies down, they will find the rest of the hundred acres?

That morning, at approximately 7.00 a.m., Shirley and I had walked to the northern cairn overlooking north field and had espied the Soays. I was inspecting them through binoculars when she nudged me to say she could see a pair of deer over by her waterhole.

I turned 180 degrees and through glasses watched them thread softly along the fence line heading for the southern pastures. If these were the pair from Northfield then, hopefully, by days end they would meet up with the other pair and our herd of Fallow would be reunited, to happily prosper in their new abode.

Once the bracken dies down their light tan colour will be easy to spot. That special morning they looked so graceful in both form and movement – an ideal compliment to the island's terrain.

On the afternoon after arriving out, on calm waters embraced with warm sun, we walked the entire island paddock by paddock. Waterholes were still full and the water table seemed high despite the days of endless sun.

I had brought a bucket of nuts hoping to attract the cattle. On reaching the old knarled elm tree I hollered and hollered. But not a sign of movement anywhere.

We therefore set off to skirt the southern reaches which were resplendent in acres of wild pinks. It was sad not seeing our flock of sheep who for five years had made this area their very own.

A PINCH OF SALTEE

A happy finding, however, was the minimum destruction by botulism. Our gull population seemed, once again, to be on the increase. Only the odd decimated body was found on our walk.

What we did notice was the unbelievable growth of grass everywhere. If the tractor had been present I could have cut acres of glorious meadow. After two years of extensive rain the best lands had been a 'bog' and no growth took place.

It was, most probably, the hot spell in spring that had germinated seeds, left dormant for the two seasons prior, that so invigorated the 2003 growth. What a bonus.

It was pastures like these that greeted us all those years ago. Our new stock will pleasure themselves in pastures new. Kerries, Soays and Fallow should have more than adequate fodder through the upcoming winters.

Back at the end of May we had the annual visit from David Cabot. Herewith his annual report of ornithological fieldwork carried out:

The storms of the winter and spring – seldom had we seen the island vegetation so "blasted" and retarded - had taken their toll of the number of breeding Fulmars. The number of occupied nest sites – each with an incubating bird – was significantly down from 276 counted in 2002 to only 187 in 2003, a decline of 32%. The largest decrease was along the west coast where there was a 43% reduction – these cliffs are the most exposed to the vagaries of the westerly storms. The southern colonies declined by 17% while the east coast fared best of all, enduring only a 13% decrease. A total of 54 adult fulmars were caught in our long polled nets and of these 38 or 70% had been ringed in previous years on the island. For comparison the retrap percentage during 2002 was 67.6%. Thus nearly three quarters of the adult population are now carrying rings providing us valuable data in this long-term study (now in its 43rd year) to understand better the population dynamics

197

A PINCH OF SALTEE

of this fascinating species. All the retraps were caught on the nest, incubating an egg. Three of the retraps had to be re-ringed as their rings had become badly abraded over time. One retraps had been ringed as an incubating adult in 1983, never retrapped until this summer, aged at least 27 years old; another had been ringed incubating an egg in 1984 and had been re-trapped breeding in 1990, 1993, 1994 and 1999 and was at least 26 years old. The final retrap had been ringed in 1999 and caught again the subsequent year.

The Cormorants, sturdier and less vulnerable to storms, fared better with a total of 367 occupied nests compared with 329 censused in 2002. We banded 214 pulli, some 9 more than last year. The birds were having a good breeding season. The number of breeding shags was 17 pairs, about the same as last year and as most were located on the east coast they had escaped most of the damaging storms. A total of 10 young shags were banded. Numbers of Razorbills and Puffins were well up to normal. We found seven carcasses of Manx shearwaters on the cliff tops along the south, west and east coasts. There was no clear villain and they were hopefully cases of normal mortality, probably inflicted by gulls. Such a number of dead birds could indicate a flourishing breeding colony. Next breeding season we will try to census the breeding numbers of Manx shearwaters. Herring gull numbers were down again and will be soon extinct as a breeding species on the island if the downward trend continues. Great black backed gulls seem more able to withstand the impact of the suspected Botulism poisoning.

As Maurice Cassidy and I were going about our work we also noticed the usual pair of Ravens, but we couldn't find their nest, if they had one. There were more breeding pairs of Oystercatchers than ever. At least three pairs Lapwings behaved as if they were holding territory and are relatively new arrivals to the island in response to the shorter grass, thanks to the herbivores. After we finished our fieldwork we scattered the ashes of the late John Barlee along the southern cliffs – he was a close personal friend of mine and had originally recommended me to visit the Saltee Islands in 1959. John was a brilliant and pioneering bird photographer (his book "Birds on the Wing", published by Collins in 1947 contains many photographs taken on the Saltees) and outstanding lecturer in Oceanography at the Royal Naval College Dartmouth for many years after graduating with First Class honours from Trinity College, Dublin. He was also an ornithological field companion of the later Major Robin Ruttledge and played a formative role in the establishment of the bird observatory on Great Saltee as well as being a frequent visitor there in the 1940s. So John is integrated into the Little Saltee ecosystem, one of the islands he loved so dearly. As we departed the island a flock of seven shelduck gave us a ceremonial fly over.

Having confidence in somebody, something, is such a weight off ones shoulders. When away from the island it has always been my policy to keep in telephonic touch with either or all of the KQ3 gang.

Paddy became the most informative as he circumvents the waters off the island every second day or so, tending his lobster pots.

He, therefore, could keep an eye on the stock and buildings for us without actually docking and setting foot.

First borns were reported by him and animals in trouble, or dead, were quite easily identified. This meant that action could be taken swiftly with prevention being the key word with regard to further tragedy.

During August 2003 it was great to hear him reply to my calls and questions as to where was he.

"Sure we're all out on the island and are about to complete the roof. It's beautiful out here and we have seen all the stock, except the deer. Everything is ok."

A PINCH OF SALTEE

Regular medical appointments are unfortunately a routine part of my life these days and keep us away from the farm at some inopportune moments.

To have the KQ3 gang looking after our interests 'in absentsia' gives us a real confidence boost.

I must reiterate, however, that it is not only the KQ3 gang but many more wonderful local farmers and residents who have a special place in their hearts for the Saltees and the little one, in particular, as it has remained quite a mystery down the centuries. Now that it is being utilised and brought back to life rekindles memories for them of their grandparents who kept alive those folklore tales of yesteryear.

All we can add to these is the respect that those great people, the Parles and Whites to mention but two, have in our minds. They were 'mighty men' achieving so much under such hardship.

We have been privileged to thread their footsteps, richly imprinted and embedded on our little acres.

As Sinatra immortalised 'we did it our way'. Yes, there were hardships, tears and sweat but all fade away to infinity when the richness of creation of life and times 'out there' is experienced. This we did. We were proud to be party to the evolution of a lifestyle some say is far gone and lost. Our pioneering efforts belie this myth. We made it actual and real.

Chimney for pot belly stove in Soay Cottage

A PINCH OF SALTEE

Chapter Twelve

REPS Inspection – Sister Deirdre – The Professor – Autignac – Glen Zaphod

September 2003 brought my second REPS inspection. This time it was Jim O'Connor who braved the voyage. But he need not have worried as Tuesday, 16th was bright, warm and the sea very, very calm. He had his 'wellies' and as an avid amateur photographer was equipped with lots of changeable telescopic lenses.

We walked every acre of 'the 100', saw the cattle, found the Soays and discovered fresh deer 'poo'. The waterholes were well filled and rivulets were moist from the 65mm of rain that had fallen in the proceeding ten days.

I was proud for Shirley and myself to have had this opportunity to show off the results of our five years of sweat and toil. Her well strimmed paths – approximately 3kms – were a strong talking point. I explained how it was more of an annual obligation to keep these well defined rather than the 70m of stone wall restoration. He agreed. We would continue with restoring walls but probably wouldn't be able to maintain the amount required in the fifty-seven days we have found to be our average annual occupation of the island.

When one thinks about that figure a significant facts comes to light. In five years we had actually only lived out there for less than three hundred days – not even a year. And yet we had achieved a full five years' workload of building, maintenance and farming projects.

On returning to Kilmore Quay Jim had a couple of other appointments which he attended to. One being the viewing of my piece of leased land and the eight Kerries that were stocked there. We, however, drove up to Dublin and prepared for our ten day

A PINCH OF SALTEE

holiday in France which commenced the following Monday. We were immensely looking forward to a much needed break.

September in ending, however, proved to be a really sad month as the day after we arrived in France we got news that my beloved sister, Deirdre, had passed away. I had been to see her on the Sunday evening before we left and I remarked, after the visit, to my niece, Valerie, that I didn't think she was 'too good'. Deirdre had been in hospital for the past ten months.

I would always get a smile out of her no matter how down I found her. Somehow this time it looked a little laboured. On kissing her forehead I said I would see her in two weeks time but she remained silent. Always she would reply "with God's help". Her brow was burning hot.

It proved impossible to get flights back in time as the funeral was held within forty-eight hours.

I found a 15th century cathedral in St. Pons de Thomieres some miles from where we were staying and spent a time meditating at the altar of the Blessed Virgin during the exact hour of her funeral service. I lit two candles and dug them into the sand filled tray as this is their method in France. No brass candelabras or candle sticks to be seen.

I knew Deirdre wouldn't have minded my absence for as siblings we both were fatalists and she especially championed 'que sera sera' – whatever will be will be.

On the Saturday evening I attended our local chapel, some 100m from the house, and was happy to be part of a Missa Cantata – but instead of sung in Latin this of course was in French!

I only wished that her last few years had been a lot different, but osteoporosis had taken a stranglehold of her frail form.

Certainly now one final piece of my island jigsaw would not be completed. It had been reserved for Deirdre and her wonderful husband of fifty-five years, Gerard Kiernan, to be

203

landed on our family hideaway and to partake of a 'braai' in the boma like they had done in South Africa, with my family, some twenty years before and loved so much.

2003 had been a particularly sad year for us both – that is Shirley and I – as I had lost one of my oldest childhood friends – John Kevany; Shirley had lost her granddaughter, Jan, and now Deirdre had departed to a more peaceful haven above.

In our herd we have Saltee Little Deirdre, a beautiful registered Kerry heifer, now hopefully in calf. My sister was delighted when I informed her, a year ago, that the best of that season's crop was named after her. She always enquired about her progress until her strength finally gave out. On every visit I would tell her about what we were working on and especially about the stock and plants.

"Any luck with the trees and shrubs?" she would continually ask. She loved trees but understood that it was virtually impossible for them to grow out on the island due to the violence of those incessant winter storms.

She kept reminding me of what Grandpa had said way back in 1941. She had a great memory, God bless her. She, to all the family, was Mother Earth. My niece, Valerie, has thankfully inherited her mother's green fingers and her own special love of the earth. She has transformed their large garden in Stillorgan into an impressionist's palette of form and colour.

The 'Professor' as I lovingly called John Kevany was indeed that at Trinity College, Dublin. He became one of the world's leading lights on the ongoing fight to curb and eradicate AIDS. We had been at Ampleforth together and during our respective lifetimes had always kept in touch. John had visited the island on a couple of occasions and I remember exceptionally well his first. It was within a couple of months of him having a hip replacement.

Unfortunately the tide was low when he and his son, Sebastian, arrived out with Declan that day. Patrick then brought them to a point as far inshore as possible depositing them on a heavily strewn shoreline of seaweed. John could not safely negotiate the slimy rocks standing up so proceeded to crawl along these outcrops until he reached a dryer section. He hadn't realised I had been clicking away with my little camera until some weeks later I presented him with a record of his visit. He wasn't too amused at first but then, as always, saw the satirical side to the event.

During that day with us he walked the entire island, bird watched, swam (out to the mooring and back no less) and finally walked upright through our dreaded rocks to the departing dinghy. His day out had so invigorated him that he kept a close watch on all our future developments and felt part of everything we tackled. John was an expert fly fisherman and spent many hours casting the western waters of Loughs Corrib and Mask. He had wished to try his expertise on our waters for sea trout and other such delectables. Sadly he never got the chance.

Autignac, a little village some twenty minutes north of Beziers in the South of France, beckoned us yet again. John and Jennifer Nicholson (Shirley's second son and daughter-in-law) had bought their retirement home in that pleasant spot surrounded by winelands in 2000.

Their house, on the Rue de la Ciffre is last in the street and looks out over hectares of vinyards. Both the houses opposite and to their east are owned by farmers who make their own wine. Next door but one is the home of Jacques Pons, Domain Fraisse – a rather large landowner. We found out, to our good fortune, that his Chardonnay 2002 was simply outstanding.

A PINCH OF SALTEE

Another extensive wine grower and near neighbour is Alain Borda whose Domain du Rouge Gorge reds and rosés had tickled our palates on previous visits. Most probably our two favourite reds hail from the Domain du Moulin de Léne and La Domain Reynardiere, both of which are situated in neighbouring villages. These wines were introduced to us by Irish friends we met in our neighbouring village Magalas. Originally from Mallow, County Cork, Nora Wells and her Chichester born husband, Douglas, had retired, after lifetimes of travelling the world, to this enchanting village and have been party to purchasing and renovating houses and flats for family members and other friends. Her brother, Gerrard Hickey, has a beautiful 'chateau' almost next to John's in Autignac, also for his retirement.

How 'small the world is' was once more brought to mind by Nora introducing Conleth and Ainya Hassett, new neighbours of hers, at a dinner party. Con hails from Bridgetown, just up the road from Kilmore Quay and Ainya is from Wexford town. Many of his relations are known to both Shirley and I and one in particular, Nicky Murphy, is one of the lobster men who keep an eye on things for us. Con is a vet and is part owner of a large practice in Northampton, the heart of the hunting Leicestershire county of England.

One of the most beautiful things about this area is the avenue of trees, mostly Plane, which engulf the kilometres of roadway leading into or out of the various towns and villages.

These canopied corridors are so pretty from spring through fall and as one wag pointed out 'they were planted by the French especially for the Germans?!' They are now luckily appreciated by one and all.

I had only seen such advanced ecological thinking in parts of India and especially so around Mysore where the British Raj planted mile upon mile of these wonderful shade trees to assist their troop movements. This was back in the nineteenth century. There arboreal legacy, both in India and in France, bears testament to forward thinking of yesteryear. I sincerely hope that our 'green'

206

friends of the twenty-first century are anyway as desirous as these illustrious ancestors.

My sister Deirdre would have marvelled at their munificence if she had been able to accompany us. All her life she loved trees, of any kind, and longed to be taken back to our former home in Mount Bellew, east Galway, which is now part of Coilte and is heavily afforested to this day. I thought of her each time we drove through these French tree lined avenues. I felt she was enjoying every leaf and branch of their existence. It all helped to cure the ache in my heart.

Autignac lies in the heart of the Faugeres district which itself is part of the Languedoc Roussillion wine region. We found great pleasure in driving from Caves to Caves, tasting this one and that and finally purchasing the one that felt right to our pallete

It was amusing to watch the locals arrive with their five and ten litre plastic containers and get filled up as at the local Total gas station. Vin Ordinaire – or plonk as we uneducated westerners refer to it, is still very much part of the everyday French life style. And long may it last. A full tank of vin ordinaire at €1.20 per litre almost matched the price of petrol.

What most of us don't realise, however, is that they rebottle this and lay it down in their darkened cellars, only to be tasted the following year. Very sensible. I remember being told to do just that in South Africa with boxes of five litre Tassenberg red purchased each time I visited certain liquor outlets. No bottle or cork was ever discarded in my household as the refilling and laying down, usually in the cupboard beneath the stairs, was a routine chore. One that was much appreciated in the months and years that followed. Buy fresh and cheap, lay it down, let it mature and appreciate its vintage. Once you get into this routine you will find you have good wine always at your table.

Earlier in the year we had spent ten days in Autignac during the pruning period which had left a sombre note as hectare after hectare offered only gnarled vine stumps on bare earth. Not a sight of beauty. It is, however, quite incredible to realise that the entire wine crop takes only four and a half months to grow, ripen and be harvested. People were saying that with the extra dry months of this summer the crop should be a vintage one. We look forward to sampling the fruits of this vintage in the coming years.

An easily managed unit of stock now exists on the island. Soays will increase in number annually and will be allowed to multiply up to regulation stocking level. Their offspring will then be sold on.

The foundation Kerry cows will hopefully produce three calves a year. These will be brought ashore at three months, heifers increasing our breeding herd and bulls being sold on.

Fallow deer will be allowed to multiply into double and treble their foundation figure. Yearling stags will then be culled and either traded on or slaughtered as organic venison.

All three species should be able to curtail the growth of bracken and rely on the acres of grassland that should be more than adequate.

On our experience of five full seasons it will be better to under graze, than over so allowing every animal a real chance of survival in no matter how bad the climate ordained that year.

The annual strimming of paths through the bracken, and then maintaining them from spring through autumn, will allow all stock access to waterholes through the lush growth of the summer months.

The pheasant population seems to maintain its numbers despite the climate and gull numbers are again on the increase. Shell duck have become quite numerous over the past three seasons and they, together with oyster catchers now cohabit our pastures.

David Cabot now has a place to stay on his annual census and ringing expedition. Over the years he has battled some fierce weather and has always had to depart in a hurry. Now, and in future years, he and his friends will be able to ease into their work schedule knowing that they have a roof over their heads and beds to sleep on if they wish to prolong their visit.

In 2004 I would like to enclose the back garden of the cottages and make the fence both stock and rabbit proof? That area could then be planted to potatoes and maize.

Our new conservatory in the west wing will hopefully supply lettuce, tomatoes, herbs and other essential veggies and flowers for both cottages.

Now that all the main buildings are roofed the prime job for the coming year is to consolidate and furnish their contents. Like a gas shower in the bathroom!

"Oh what bliss", I hear in Shirley's pleading tone!

A few large pvc tanks are needed, lengths of guttering and a little pump should do the trick. It sounds so simple after all the major tasks we have undertaken in these years of refurbishment.

Perhaps dreams do come true and ambitions do get achieved. These will not be for the want of trying and what an educational, inspirational project it has been.

Probably one of the nicest and most rewarding aspects of farming – pedigree farming – is to be able to plot the future and see ones labours spread throughout that breed society.

I chose Kerry cattle as I knew they had been on the islands in the centuries before this present one. Little did I know, at the same time, that another Kerry herd was being farmed on Clear Island off the south-west Cork coast. And little did I realise that the union of these two bloodlines would take place in this novella's time scale.

Having decided to retain three Kerry ladies on the island I now needed a young bull for the 2004 season. My ladies were having a sabbatical in 2003/2004.

Raymonde Hilliard once again came to my rescue and told me about Capt. Duncan McLachlan's Glen Herd at Cape Clear. She had recently visited the island to inspect his senior bull with a

A PINCH OF SALTEE

view to it being used for the National AI (artificial insemination) bank. She had also seen a four month old bull calf by him which could be for sale. The blood lines she told me would be a perfect outcross.

After a few island to island cell phone calls agreement was reached and my latest purchase – Glen Zaphod – was ferried from Cape Clear (nine kilometres out) to Baltimore, then Skibereen where we collected him. We had a long day ahead of us – Clonakilty, Cork, Waterford, across in the ferry at Passage East to Kilmore Quay and finally out on *the banana boat* to Little Saltee.

That's called island hopping!!

He can stay out on Little Saltee for many reproductive years ahead. Perhaps, at times, Glen Zaphod will, with wistful eyes, search on a clear day across Hook Head and hope to catch a glimpse of his original island home. Wishful thinking I know but isn't that what life is all about?

I know that our five year project was peppered with outlandish ideas. But if you don't try you will never know. We have been repaid, many times over, upon fulfilment of our enterprise.

> *I am haunted by numberless islands, and many a Danaan shore,*
> *Where time would surely forget us, and Sorrow come near us no more;*
> *Soon far from the rose and the lily and fret of the flames would we be,*
> *Were we only white birds, my beloved, buoyed out on the foam of the sea!*

(W.B.Yeats, *The White Birds*)

A PINCH OF SALTEE